WHEN LITTLE BECAME MUCH

A JOURNEY FROM OBSCURITY TO SIGNIFICANCE

CLIFTON L. TAULBERT

"The life I remembered from my small hometown became the stories God gently pulled from my heart for a book that would set me on the course of discovering my place within His plan. I feel as if I have relived the story of the young lad who gave to Jesus his five loaves and two fishes and marveled at how the Master's touch caused little to become much."

WHEN LITTLE BECAME MUCH: A Journey From Obscurity to Significance

ISBN: 0-924748-63-X
UPC: 88571300033-8

Printed in the United States of America
© 2005 by Clifton L. Taulbert

Milestones International Publishers
4410 University Dr., Ste. 113
Huntsville, AL 35816
(256) 536-9402, ext. 234; Fax: (256) 536-4530
www.milestonesintl.com

1 2 3 4 5 6 7 8 9 10 11 / 09 08 07 06 05

DEDICATION

In memoriam: Elna Peters Boose

My great-aunt, who by opening both her heart and her home became God's partner in shaping my life and preparing me for a future that is still unfolding.

1894–1981

CONTENTS

Prologue .vii

Preface xi

Chapter 1   From a Small Front Room...
I Started My Journey 1

Chapter 2   Drawing the Short Straw in Las Vegas . .13

Chapter 3   Phil Donahue...New York City 25

Chapter 4   The Governor's Mansion...
On the Inside, Looking Out 39

Chapter 5   Speaking in the Rotunda of the
United States Capitol 47

Chapter 6   A Plantation Called Glen Mary...
Dwelling Together in Unity 55

Chapter 7   Beyond Greenfield...Hitler's Germany . .69

Chapter 8   Speaking in the Presence of Justice . . .79

Chapter 9   Costa Rica...Brother Cliff,
Can You Come? 91

Chapter 10   Scholars and Educators 107

Chapter 11   Irish Mayors and Kenyan Delegates . .119

Chapter 12   China's Hong Kong...
Beyond the Delta Turn Roads 129

Chapter 13   God's Chosen People in My Story 139

Chapter 14   Fragments Feeding the
Next Generation 151

Chapter 15   Discovering My Place...
A Continuous Journey 161

About the Author 175

PROLOGUE

Thank you for choosing to walk into my world, the Mississippi Delta. I was born during the era of legal segregation. World War II was over and life in the American South had changed very little. "Jim Crow"—the system that supported legal segregation—was firmly entrenched. It was no different in my small hometown of Glen Allan, Mississippi. It was a cotton community where most of what we did was defined by that world. It was in that world of rigid laws and social restrictions that my life began. The difficulties of growing up in such an environment are well documented, from restricted social movement to hideous acts of racism. Yet it was there among the people I call the "porch people"—ordinary people who used their front porches to welcome our lives, to hold their informal meetings, and yes, to dream about our future—that I also experienced an incredible sense of community. God showed up in the unselfishness of the ordinary people who became extra-ordinary leaders in the stories that I would write into best-selling cultural biographies.

My first book, *Once Upon a Time When We Were Colored*, captured the imagination of the world and clearly showed the power of God's presence, even during the worst of our times. Our Senate Foreign Relations Department included it in the gift package provided to Nelson Mandela upon his release from prison. From my early world of material scarcity where even the libraries were closed to me, God called me to become a writer. And along the way, I was nominated for the Pulitzer Prize and became one of the first African-Americans to receive the Mississippi Institute of Art and Letters Award for Non-Fiction Literature. I saw my first book be made into a major motion picture, but most important of all, I have witnessed the world's response to the principles of building community that grew out of my book, *Eight Habits of the Heart*, which *USA TODAY* hailed as their year-end choice of books to enrich our minds and lives. From being one of CNN's Millennium Minutes for community to lecturing before United States Supreme Court judges, I know of a certainty that when we give our "little" to God, it does indeed become "much."

For those of you who have never traveled south to the Delta and may not know all the terms we embrace, I want to provide you a conversation of clarification so that you can feel as if you are one of us while reading this book. First, I want to explain the name and title, "Ma Ponk." She is my great-aunt whose legal name is Mrs. Elna Peters Boose. She raised me and within her home I saw her faith lived out on a daily basis. Now you can call her your great-aunt as well. All the other names and titles will be readily understood. Again, when you see the term *porch people*, just remember it is a collective term for the African-American people of my community who welcomed and took care of me.

So that you don't have to go to your map unless you choose to do so, the Mississippi Delta is that rich triangular mass of land covering west central Mississippi and over into Arkansas. It was called the Delta due to its shape and the richness of the soil from all the flooding of the mighty Mississippi over centuries. Glen Allan itself is located in Washington County just 28 miles south of Greenville, Mississippi, off Highway Number One where one of America's prettiest lakes, Lake Washington, is found.

You also will see the term *juke joint*. This is the colloquial name for what you would call a restaurant-bar today—a place where greasy food was served and the blues were played. And if you run across *turn road*, don't stop reading. It simply means the dirt access road that separated the fields, the place where farmers turned their tractors and housed their trailers. A *gunnysack* is a term used to define sacks that held corn and other feed.

Thank you for coming home with me and experiencing the hand and heart of God during my life while growing up in the Mississippi Delta, then traveling with me on a journey that only He could have arranged.

Clifton Taulbert's first grade picture at the Glen Allan school.

Clifton Taulbert speaking at a medical school's "white coat" ceremony.

PREFACE

In small cotton communities during the early part of the 20th century, African-American preachers often kept our spirits alive with Sunday morning sermons where we were told, in dramatic terms, the power of our God to be sufficient in the midst of lack. No story was more compelling than the one described in chapter 6 of the gospel of Saint John. As a little kid nestled between my great-aunt and her friends who occupied the "mother's bench," I heard again and again the story that would eventually be descriptive of my life. I never dreamed, though, that this biblical story would somehow come alive in my life and that I would be given an opportunity to witness the touch that would, over time, set me on a course of finding my place within God's plan.

How could I ever forget the story? The preacher made it come alive. It was as if I was right there with the little boy, no older than me. I listened and imagined a small boy in blue jeans and a plaid shirt making his way among the crowd tightly holding on to his brown paper bag lunch of fried catfish and bread. I had no concept of Jewish food, but I knew fish and catfish were the sandwiches I ate. As the preacher preached, he left us with the picture of the crowd getting bigger and bigger. According to the Scriptures, Jesus had become very popular and as such drew a crowd. So powerful and compelling were His words that people followed Him wherever He went. Without the comfort of hotels and fast food outlets and inner-city bus systems, they walked and in some cases ferried themselves across the Sea of Galilee to be with Jesus, to listen as He talked, and to marvel at the miracles He performed and they witnessed. And with each "Praise God" and shout from our preacher, he let us know that the crowd was also getting hungry.

Both the gospel of John and our preacher from back home left us with the knowledge that Jesus was personally moved by the crowd, 5,000 men plus women and children. He also realized their human need for food. So He posed the question to His disciple Philip, *"Whence shall we buy bread, that these may eat?"* (verse 5) At our little Baptist church back home in Glen Allan, we were taught that when God asks a question, He already knows the answer.

Philip, the disciple, answered that their money was not enough to buy food for such a crowd. Andrew, another one of the disciples, perhaps rather sarcastically or maybe just emphasizing the size of the problem, said, "We do have a young lad with five loaves of bread and two fishes." Jesus knew that. However, it was that statement of the reality of what was present that changed the course of their day. In the natural process of things, five loaves of bread and two fishes mean absolutely nothing; however, when in the presence of Jesus, little becomes much.

I know it must have been a surprise to the disciples when Jesus responded positively to Andrew's casual answer. Rather than debating the logic of Andrew's response, Jesus began the miracle. Jesus had them act immediately to prepare for a feast that was nowhere in sight. This must have taken a lot of "faith" on the disciples' part. Why count and arrange and prepare the people to have a meal when the obvious reality is there is "not enough"? How long did it take them to count? And what answers would they give as to the menu? I'm sure they were asked. The people could see that no food was readily available. In the midst of their thoughts as to how such a feat could be accomplished, they obeyed Jesus.

Jesus took what the young lad had as his own personal lunch, brought it to His hands and heart, and gave thanks. In so doing, everything changed.

He began to distribute from a sack lunch a meal that fed 5,000 men and the additional women and children. After all had eaten their fill, Jesus commanded the disciples to go a step further and, where once there was just enough for one, 12 baskets of leftovers were gathered—fragments from His touch.

I never thought my stories to be of international consequence. I thought the small book I had written to be no more than a personal legacy of memories for me, my family, and maybe a few friends. In 1990, calls of congratulations were coming from all over the country from friends and acquaintances I had not seen for years. My very first book, *Once Upon a Time When We Were Colored*, had been favorably reviewed by *The New York Times*. Shortly to follow was an in-depth review by *The Boston Globe* and the subsequent calls from L.A. film agents.

This small volume published in 1989 by a virtually unknown Midwestern publishing company had captured the imagination of the media around the country. Not only had the book made an inroad into the secular media, but it also had landed me a front cover story on *The Pentecostal Evangel*. I was interviewed on "The 700 Club" and was a guest on the Moody Radio Program. The United States Senate Foreign Relations Committee had requested an autographed copy for Nelson Mandela, recently released from prison. And in 1996, *Once Upon a Time When We Were Colored* became a major motion picture garnering two thumbs up and winning acclaim at the NAACP Image Awards and The Movie Guide Awards, a Christian organization committed to decency within the film industry.

While the world—even the country of Israel—celebrated the book and the film, I found the international acceptance rather difficult to believe. After all, I had only written about a very small cotton community, a place where regular people stepped up and surrounded my life. Little did I know that the widespread acceptance had little to do with me, but all to do with God, His plan, and His touch. From one small book, God started an incredible literary journey and an international conversation on the issues of community. Just like the little boy of the Bible, I gave God what I had and watched as it multiplied in my presence.

This is a picture of one of the many fields where Clifton Taulbert, his parents, grandparents and great-grandparents worked in the Mississippi Delta. It is in Issaquena County in a place still called the "Colored Colony." According to Taulbert, God called forth for the stories for the nations from such a place.

From a pasteboard box of short stories written while Taulbert was a soldier in the 1960's, books and essays continue to emerge, filling the life and hearts of thousands around the world. Taulbert calls them his Southern Door.

Chapter 1

FROM A SMALL FRONT ROOM...I STARTED MY JOURNEY

For me, it all started so long ago in the Mississippi Delta, first with my great-grandparents and then with my great-aunt, Ma Ponk, in her small front room. I was cared for by my aging aunt who was determined that I would have enough for my life's journey. In all that I encountered, it was her love and acts of kindness that moved my life along in spite of the rigors of our segregated rural life that defined our day.

Her life and the life of unselfishness that I experienced from others became the small lunch of memories that would eventually be placed in the hands of God.

Ma Ponk, as she was affectionately called, probably had no idea that God had chosen her to be part of His much bigger plan. I was just the great-nephew who needed a place to stay and a bed to call my own. Even her willingness to take on this extra burden would become part of an answer to a question posed by a world that yearned to know the look and feel of community—a place where reaching out to others is expected and welcomed, creating "hope" within our uncertain times.

Ma Ponk's small front room, along with the front porches of numerous others, became the place where hearts and hands would come together for such a time as this. We all were where we should have been, and so was God. He was in the Mississippi Delta working behind the scenes in the hearts of the people who had their own burdens to bear, but who chose not to overlook their brothers and sisters.

How could I forget the circumstances of my birth to an unmarried schoolgirl? How could I forget the picture etched in my mind of Ma Ponk on her knees night after night? I could not forget, and God remembered.

Growing up in Glen Allan, Mississippi, I somehow knew that the "way" God was making for Ma Ponk, me, our friends, and other family members was connected to my great-aunt's nightly ritual of kneeling to pray before we climbed into our beds. Listening as she had her nightly conversation with an unseen friend—and it was indeed a conversation—I drifted off to sleep with the reassurance of her words that "now everything's gonna be jus' fine."

As I experienced the largess of their hearts, I had no dream of their daily lives extending beyond the cotton fields of the Delta. Looking back at the world of my youth, I marvel at the path God made for me through the goodness of these ordinary people—Ma Mae, Uncle Cleve,

Poppa Joe, Mama Pearl, Mother Luella Byrd, and so many others. Ma Ponk, though, was the one God chose to shepherd my life, and I'm glad He did.

Because Ma Ponk willingly allowed God to use her life to salvage my own, many good and lasting seeds continue to bring a rich harvest.

Within the restricted world of cotton and racism where I grew up, becoming a recognized writer was not among the daily dreams of young black boys and girls. You must understand that when I was a child, the library in my small hometown was closed to me—a handicap over which I had no control. I didn't grow up embracing great authors, much less wishing to become one. Yet, today, I have an ISBN number and am catalogued in the Library of Congress. Books that I have penned now grace the shelves of the library that was once closed to me.

My books were simply the everyday memories of a small boy, nothing spectacular or out of the ordinary. The roads we traveled were often dirt and graveled, and field-work defined the adult world I knew. Everybody knew each other and kinship was treasured. We were "colored" children growing up among our own in a broader world that never took the time to know who we really were. These were *my* memories, my very own. Even as I wrote them in the quietness of night in a military barracks far from my home, I thought they were just for me—stories to ease my fear of being sent to Viet Nam.

I was reluctant to write my first book. I remember my very first story. I wrote it while in the Air Force and though I felt good while writing it, afterwards I questioned its value beyond my heart. I wrote about my *love for my great-grandfather and how I missed being in the warm world that he had created for me. Later, I kept asking myself, **Who'd want to read about an aging African-American whose 1949 Buick always broke down?** I honestly thought that I had nothing of value to say to the world. Somehow the memory of the kindnesses, the small acts of unselfishness that I saw and experienced, kept filling my head night after night. I wrote just to have peace of mind. In due season, God would call for all that I had written.*

At the time I was writing, His plan for my memories was not revealed to me. His plans for me were far beyond the fields of the Mississippi Delta. He used the stories from my life to become modern-day parables of His power to preserve community within the hearts and lives of a beleaguered people, the African-Americans of the Mississippi Delta. God knew that in the days, years, decades, and the new century I would welcome, people would need to have parables of unselfishness from lives they recognized.

God was using me, but He was thinking about others. Jesus was thinking of the thousands when He received all that the young lad had to offer. He still looks out for others and chooses to use us in the process. He used the willing hearts and hands that lifted me to reveal the look and feel of community and the requirements to build and maintain one, even in the midst of great obstacles. God continues to look out for His children even when we have no idea of what we want or what we need. And He still gives us an opportunity to join with Him.

Driven by unselfishness, these ordinary people—cousins, aunts, uncles, grandparents, and neighbors—set out to help me find the gift that He wishes for all of us to have and share. From their voices I learned to stay out of trouble, away from childish behavior that could have branded one for life. Without their volunteering into my upbringing, I could have been bruised and scarred by the presence of racism and bigotry. They shielded my life from that as much as they could. Their faith sustained them and developed the unselfishness that I would need. While in their midst, I never gave a second thought to their ways of doing things. I accepted their gifts as ordinary, yet today it seems as if this very ordinary type of living has come up as a memorial to their God.

From the small front room in Glen Allan, Mississippi, to St. Louis, and to the Air Force, at last I was in the place God would use to draw the stories out of my memory. Stationed in the military during the Viet Nam war was an unlikely place and an unlikely time to write heart-warming stories. But this was the place the writing started, a place I had not planned on being. Being a soldier happened, but God was in the choice I made.

In 1964, the year after I graduated from high school and moved to St. Louis, the local St. Louis news was dominated by the Viet Nam war. It overshadowed everything else. While eating dinner, the counting of bodies could be over-heard from the radios or televisions. Nearly all my male friends over 18 were being sent off to Viet Nam. I knew I would be next in line.

I didn't have the soldier mentality. Even while growing up in the South where hunting game was mandatory for all boys, I flunked hunting. The prospect of being drafted into the Army was frightening. Even though I was a long ways from my native home, I nevertheless kept my contact with the church. Prayer was never too far from me. As a child, I had learned the value of prayer. In my innocence, I prayed for God to make a way for me. He did. The very next morning after I honestly prayed, I walked up Grand Avenue in St. Louis and enlisted in the United States Air Force. Two days later, I received notification to report to the nearest Army recruiting station. I thank God for directing my path and am so thankful that I acted upon His small voice.

I made it through basic training and technical school with honors, even passing marksmanship with honors. After technical school, I was permanently assigned to Dow Air Force Base in Bangor, Maine. It was cold and remote, but just the sort of place God would use to start me on His journey. While I was writing in Bangor, I had friends dying in Viet Nam. There was so much pain. Nevertheless, I felt this compelling need to take every spare minute of my time and write about the folks I remembered from back home.

With the constant reminders of war and the loss of friends, the writing soon became an escape for me. It was comforting for me to write of home as we faced times of great cultural crisis within our country. At first I thought I was writing these short stories to pass the time and to keep my mind off being sent to the front lines of the war in Viet Nam. Now I know I was not just passing time. The mission had begun. God had taken me from St. Louis to the military during a time when reflecting on home would be of great value. As I write this, I am laughing to myself. I know if I had stayed in St. Louis, I never would have written the book. It was

*necessary for me to be in this place of emotional con-
flict so that I could recall with clarity the unselfishness
that was the ordinary people I knew and loved. Yes,
while my life was in the midst of war, God asked me
to write stories of peace and comfort.*

On those cold nights in Bangor, Maine, I would write,
and as I wrote the sound of the home folks' laughter and the
memory of their voices would drown out my fears. During
my writing time, I would again be safe at home, far from the
possibilities of being sent to battle. God would take me back
to the place where I first encountered unselfishness and
compassion, and both looked like people—people I knew
well. He needed those stories because He knew what they
would mean to a society being defined by personal greed,
personal gratification, and the bits and bites of advancing
technology.

*Who would expect timeless and universal stories
of a compassionate community to come from a small
village in the Mississippi Delta during the era of legal
segregation? That's the power of God. His presence
makes the difference. Yielded vessels are all that God
requires. Your "place" does not dictate God's action.
He will use what we have and will start where we are.*

All through my military career, I wrote the stories that
sprang from my heart. After my military career ended in
August of 1968, the writing continued even on into college
and through graduation in 1971 from Oral Roberts
University. Night after night and year after year, I stole time
from my life and wrote about everyday people from my
hometown, recalling with clarity our shared life stories,
adding more Mississippi Delta stories to the brown pasteboard box that lived under my bed—many of which had

been rejected by some of the finest publications in America.

In 1988, while sifting through the short stories, I reflected with great fondness upon the world that my great-aunt had provided me. I originally experienced the richness of writing in her home. Nearly every Saturday morning I watched and listened as she read and wrote letters as if she were handling great literary works. In our small cotton community, letters were immensely important, keeping us connected with worlds beyond the Delta and expanding the reach of our small homes. Listening as Ma Ponk read and responded to the letters she received, I grew up sensing the importance of reading and writing.

In that simple setting so long ago, God was preparing me for a much bigger job—one that would not begin to materialize until some three decades later while I served as a soldier in the military. (That's the value of honestly looking back; you will most likely find that God was there all the time working through ordinary people to accomplish His divine plans—without consulting us.) The stories written during my four-year enlistment ended up in a box under my bed. I couldn't get rid of them. They traveled with me. But it's good to know that God's timing eventually comes.

Some 24 years after the start of my writing while in the military, the political climate in America changed—and so had the demands of the literary world. But 1988 was on God's calendar. In the fullness of time, after I had given up and said that my stories would never be published, God opened up an unusual publishing door at just the right time. His touch continued. The publishing company was small, barely regional, so I still thought that the published book would only reach me, my family, and a few friends.

*I knew I had not written **War and Peace** and saw my collection of short stories as limited to a specific time and to the interest of a specific group of people. I was not privy to God's plan. I was simply following my heart.*

Now in 1989, 25 years after I started the process, the small cardboard box of stories that I had kept under my bed and carried with me from military base to military base and all through my remaining college years, became a book.

From His hands a book was born. I had given up, but God was still working on my behalf. I had endured so many rejections early on, but now the right season had come. From today's perspective, I see this as one of many significant catalysts for the start of my journey finding my place within His plan.

I had no thoughts of anything timeless and universal coming from my small community onto the table of the literary world.

Glen Allan, my small and insignificant hometown becoming the theme of a book makes me think even more of the young boy and his small lunch. Surely he must have wondered if Jesus and His crew knew what they were doing when he was asked to bring his humble lunch to solve a massive hunger crisis. But once in God's hands, the small and insignificant personal lunch became the feast that fed thousands with 12 baskets left over and that continues to nourish us today. As the years would pass, I would see this same scenario in my own life as well.

I watched as God took a cardboard box of stories, lifted them up, and blessed them into many books, lectures, a movie, and countless conversations for waiting hearts in a generation of people far removed from the Mississippi Delta of the 1950's. He brings a meal just in time for a new century in need of a caring community.

Yes, *Once Upon a Time When We Were Colored* against all odds became an overnight success in Tulsa, totally shattering the statement from my publishers that the 3,000 books printed would last five years. Tulsa's acceptance started the process that changed the course of my life and the thoughts and attitudes of thousands around the world. From the bright lights of Las Vegas to the capitals of Europe, I would find myself in a world beyond anything I could have dreamed or planned. Because God asked me to give Him my memories, the porch people of the Mississippi Delta became more than field hands, sharecroppers, and tractor drivers; they became a small cotton community not to be forgotten, a place where God showed up and instituted timeless principles of unselfishness—the power within community.

It came out from beneath a basket of obscurity, an unquenchable light of faith and faithfulness in one boy's life, spilling over now for others to read and experience God among us. When God invites you into His plans, everything changes. The roadblocks and barriers no longer hold you captive.

And now you too can travel with me on the many roads that were beyond Ma Ponk's front room window and see the hand of God once again using simple stories to reveal His presence in all the circumstances of our lives. Being a guest in Las Vegas of all places, the biggest juke joint I had ever seen, started my travels that continue today. Yes, it was there amidst the neon lights of Las Vegas, as a breakfast keynote speaker to thousands, that I experienced God. Thousands heard my voice, but I know who was talking.

God had begun His good work and would continue.

Fragments From His Touch...
Life Lessons to Pass Along

God will not leave us where He finds us. This is our eternal hope and present blessing. Our circumstances, no matter how dire, do not deter His stooping to lift our lives. This likewise is His example for us to do the same for others. God knows where we are. And in His time, He takes us out of the danger to a safe place where care and redemption abound.

In the midst of racism and all it offered, He provided me a safe place—a caring environment where I saw His heart at work. He often calls out to people like us, just as He did to my great-aunt, to step up and become part of His plan.

In return, He ensures that our unselfish acts extend far beyond the day and time in which we reached out.

Chapter 2

DRAWING THE SHORT STRAW IN LAS VEGAS

After the initial success of the book in Tulsa, which shocked and surprised all of us, I was prepared to be a short-lived local celebrity. But while I was basking in lights that I felt would soon be dimmed, plans were underway in New York that would set the stage for the direction my life would take. It was happening outside of my knowledge and without input from me. At that time I was in the banking industry and never figured to be far removed from that world. For me, being in corporate America was God's will for my life. My world, though, was on the verge of change, and the change was being led by forces beyond me.

I never dreamed that I'd walk into God's "will" for my life while in Las Vegas, and yet it was there in a crowded room at the Las Vegas Hilton that God showed up. I had little choice but to take notice. The invitation to my small

13

publisher to provide an author to speak at the prestigious Booksellers' Breakfast was a miracle within itself. I had never spoken in public, and my book was barely known. In all honesty, we were still searching for the defining attributes of the book. The American Booksellers Association (ABA) had always pulled their speakers from the pool of authors with the New York publishers. We all were excited at the invitation, but it would be much later before I realized that my memories of unselfishness, my five loaves and my two fishes that I gave to Him, would become big enough to feed thousands.

Just being invited to Las Vegas overwhelmed me. I was excited and cautious. After all, I had grown up in a rather conservative religious household where this type of activity had little or no place. As I thought about my upcoming trip to Vegas, I felt as if I was somehow slipping in the back door of Mr. James Gaston's Glen Allan Café. In order to understand my concerns, let me take you back to my hometown's version of Las Vegas.

Like most of the young people in my small community, I too was intrigued by Mr. James Gaston's Café and the neon lights that set it apart. Back home, the few neon lights we did see were captivating, and no place was more captivating than the Café, commonly known as the juke joint—the "good times" place. At night, the otherwise plain building came to life with the few neon signs beckoning all who passed by to come on in and stay a spell. Even from the road where I was destined to stand and watch, I could smell the greasy hamburgers and fries doing their best to invite me in. As a young boy, I would see the women who by day had worked in the fields, but who now, cleaned up and pressed, were beautiful. I would watch as they and their alluring laughter walked by me and slowly walked in.

I was intrigued, but my great-aunt with whom I lived was not having any of that. As much as I wanted to walk into the mystery of the lights that turned our rather dull days into the possibilities of fun-filled nights, I was unable to do so. I could see the lights from the outside, but Ma Ponk was having no part of my becoming part of the neon world of captivating women, beer, cigarettes, and more beer.

Mr. Gaston's Café would forever remain a mystery as Ma Ponk and her faith partnered to keep me on the outside looking in.

So decades later, no longer a young boy but a full-grown man with his first book published, I was no longer on the outside. The doors in Las Vegas had opened wide, and I would be part of an international audience of writers and booksellers. This was indeed an honor, and I now know that it was part of a much bigger plan.

Looking back more than ten years later from my Las Vegas visit, I can clearly see the blessings of the hand of God on my career as a writer and lecturer. My invitation to the ABA made no sense. No one knew me. My book had not yet found its place in America. And my virtually unknown publishers were from the Midwest, not New York City. Yet, they invited my small press and their unknown author to be part of this international breakfast program with booksellers and literary guests from around the world.

To follow God's leading can sometimes be scary, but if you listen closely and walk humbly before Him, one day you will look back and see ordered steps.

As more information about the event came to my publishers and I, my fears mounted as I imagined myself standing before such a large audience for the very first time in my life. I was scared. They wanted me to talk about the small town and the ordinary people, my family and friends from Washington County. In the book, I felt them to be safe. I was unsure as to how they would sound when marched out into a world so foreign to their simple lifestyle. Yet, this was the task before me, to take the audience to the Mississippi Delta and introduce to them the folk who stopped along the way to take good care of me and, in so doing, became the memories of unselfishness that I cherish.

We arrived at night, and needless to say, both my wife Barbara and I were overwhelmed with all that this desert city had to offer, the neon lights notwithstanding. However, none of this visual excitement could ease my fear as I thought about the big breakfast and the morning speech that I had to deliver. That night while my wife and I were sitting in our hotel room looking out at a sea of bright multicolored lights, I decided that I should call my mother for prayer. She had been excited about the book from the very beginning, always assuring me that God was in the middle of the writing. I accepted her thoughts but felt as if I was writing the book, not God. I had been raised in the church, but over the years and with much travel and schooling, my simple "faith" was not as it should have been. That night, however, I needed the calming that I knew prayer could bring.

My mother Mary was by all standards a prayer warrior and just the right person to reach God on our behalf. Though I was privy to all that the ABA and Las Vegas had to offer, I knew in my heart what I really needed. Without God I'd be on my own, and I didn't want that. I wanted Him on board with me.

Mother had come to know the fullness of God when she found her life to be at the point of death. According to her and her doctors, she was rescued from death, and no one knew this better than mother. Upon her return home from Greenville, Mississippi's King Daughter's Hospital, she made a commitment to God that changed the course of all our lives. I was just eleven years old at the time, but I recall the day my mother's life was filled with the power of God's presence. It was a sovereign move of the Holy Spirit. We lived off the beaten path and our lives did not encounter itinerant preachers with the latest message. All we had was what we had known all our lives. However, while in the King Daughter's Hospital, my mother's conversation with God opened a door that we had not known. My mother and her best friend honestly prayed to God to give them all He had for their lives. He heard their prayers, and in a rather miraculous way their lives were changed. Without the blessings of learned teachers, I witnessed these two best friends seeking God as well as His answering their prayers. It was in that setting that I too came to know Jesus and to understand that He was fully capable of doing just what He said He would do. Nevertheless, over the years what had once been sweet and precious began to get in the way of all my accomplishments, and I began to lean to my own understanding and to embrace my own way. But I had not forgotten the God of Glen Allan and my mother who had always kept in close contact with Him. So there in Las Vegas I knew immediately what I needed. I needed to tap into my mother's commitment and her faith.

That night in Vegas I called Mommy and God answered. I remembered His faithfulness. I had seen it in Glen Allan. When it seemed that all would fail, Mother would pray and God would answer. When racism raised its head, Mother would pray and I would witness as dyed-in-the-wool racists did the right thing.

17

I knew God and had seen His awesome power, but I would, over the years, define my own way of serving Him. But as you will see, the God I encountered in Glen Allan had not changed, and many years later I would face Him again.

We finally reached Mother, and after telling her about the city and how all the clubs reminded me of Mr. James Gaston's place—only a million times bigger—I asked her to pray with us. She did. I remember holding the phone tightly and wishing that she was in the room with us, but as she confidently prayed, after a while I could feel the assurance and the calmness I needed. In those brief moments, I thought that maybe things would really be all right. I'll never forget her prayers and how she assured me that God would show up the next morning and that He would do well and we all would see and know. My mother had learned to trust God over the years in her life, and that night she imparted her sense of trust into us. My wife and I both felt relieved as we hung up the phone. Even though I was still unsure as to how tomorrow would turn out, I was left somewhat assured that, somehow, God was in Las Vegas and that He would be with me the next morning.

In the morning, dressed and walking by myself, I headed to the "Green Room" where I would meet the other guests who would share the morning with me. My wife had already gone to the breakfast location where she would meet my cousin Joe and his wife Clara. Confident that Barbara was settled, I took my time finding my way to the Green Room. It gave me time to think and pray privately as I walked the long corridors in search of the room. I finally found the right place. Showing the usher the required credentials, I was welcomed into a room where I stood with my mouth open as I looked into the faces of Donald Trump, Angela Lansbury, Isabella Allende, and the late Cleveland Amory, just to drop a few names.

I sat with Isabelle Allende and finally found words to join in the conversation. Everything was going well until the question was asked as to who would be the first to speak. No one volunteered, so they decided to draw straws. I had never drawn straws in my life, and to my surprise and shock I drew the shortest straw. I was chosen as the first one to speak. I really needed God. All the fear I thought I had dropped along the way showed up, and all I could do was nod to the others with approval.

While all the others laughed and talked among themselves, I sat fairly quiet as my heart thumped louder and louder. I just wanted everything to be over, but how could it be when we had not yet begun? Finally, seemingly out of nowhere, a young man appeared and requested that we follow him to the ballroom. We all did, and of course I was near the front, sweating and trying to recall all that God had promised the night before. The closer I got to the ballroom, the more I wanted to have God as my very present PR person standing there with me, holding my hand. As I passed by the hordes of slot machines, I began to ask myself if God really would show up in such a city. At that moment, nothing looked like the churches I had known as the houses of God.

My fear was real, even though the book actually was published, something I had once thought would never happen. At this moment, I must have been like the young lad with his loaves of bread and his two fish, thinking to himself that maybe he should have stayed at home. I couldn't take the book back. It had been assigned an ISBN number. It was already in the Master's hands, but I was afraid of what would not happen. My book looked so small alongside the publications of the other speakers.

I could imagine the "Andrews" of my day talking among themselves about my small and unknown book, even questioning its presence beside the more notable books and recognized people.

Upon entering the ballroom, I was overwhelmed. I was without words. The place was packed with people, thousands of people, and only three African-Americans: my wife and my two cousins. I tried to catch their eyes, but no such luck. I could see them, but with the crowd so big, it was difficult for the four of us to "eye" each other, so I followed the procession and found my place on stage. From this vantage point, my sense of uneasiness was even greater. Sitting down and looking over the crowd, it seemed even larger. Each author was flanked by a member of their publishing team, as was I. And it was good that I was, in that I suddenly became incredibly nervous and seemed as if I was a candidate for fainting. My publisher, noticing the change in my face, leaned over and whispered these words in my ear: "Whatever you do, don't die until your speech is over."

In the moment that I needed human encouragement, my own publisher added to my fear and trepidation. I felt alone and knew I really needed God to show up. I tried not to look on the crowd. It was getting bigger and whiter all the time, and all I had to offer was a sack lunch of memories from a predominantly African-American community somewhere in the Mississippi Delta, a place that none of them had ever been or planned to go.

Sweating and still nervous, I took his advice and decided to live. However, it was rather difficult to hold on to my resolve. As I looked at the others, watching the media hover over Donald Trump and Angela Lansbury, I wondered if God was nearby with His camera crew. I really felt alone as I contemplated addressing this massive audience about a time and place in America when a race of people was called "colored." I felt as if my small stories had no place in such an international audience. Would they understand the people who had cared for me? Would they snicker at their "funny" sounding names? Would I lose my train of thought? Would I embarrass my wife and cousins? As these real questions raced through my mind, the preliminaries came to an end and I was being introduced. While my bio was being read, I was reliving the previous night and the prayer my mother had prayed. She had assured me that God would show up, but up to now I was feeling all alone. I was not feeling or seeing God. In my moments of trying to rid myself of the fear, instead of concentrating on what I had to do and what was being said at the podium, I was counting people—and the numbers were big. Very big. However, no one else was counting and before I knew it, I heard my name being called to address the audience. I heard the words: "Welcome Clifton Taulbert."

It was as if I had been singled out to give my lunch to this hungry crowd. These people were professionals. Many had spent all their lives reading and critiquing the works of others. I know they were trying to figure out who I was and where I had come from. And it didn't help that they had never heard of my publisher. I had little choice other than to get up and make my way to the podium, now vacant and waiting to be filled by me.

With nowhere to run or hide, I slowly stood up and made my way to the podium. Holding tightly to the sides, I opened my mouth and began a conversation that I now know God placed within my heart. I'll never forget how it all happened and how quickly.

I looked out on the audience and posed a question that had, for all practical purposes, just jumped into my head. "Where does hope live?" And it was as if the conversation was leading me. I could hear myself talking, but the trip was being led by someone I could not see. Within my heart, though, I could understand.

I gave them what I had: five small loaves and two fishes of memories. God had asked for these memories many years ago and now He was preparing to show me what happens when we trust all that we are to Him.

I took them to Glen Allan and to the people who, through their unselfish living, became the "hope" I needed. I am not sure when God checked in, but I'll forever live with the reality that He was there and that I saw and felt His presence for myself. No tape exists of the presentation, even though it was being filmed by a professional camera crew, who by some accounts became so taken by the presentation that they forgot to do their job. As I talked about my world and the people who became the hope I needed for my life to be sustained, it seemed as if God took my words and gave them wings. By the time I was finished, thousands were literally on their feet. They cheered. They cried. They embraced my life. They embraced me.

I now know how the young lad must have felt when he saw his meager meal yielding such return in his presence. Just think—a small sack lunch had become the answer to a potential hunger crisis. And I was seeing it again. The stories were feeding hearts in ways I had not dreamed.

And I no longer feared as I stood trembling with thankfulness...that my God showed up as He said He would, even in Las Vegas. I knew that what I had written and now had said was of value beyond my small world. He had indeed blessed my lunch—ordinary memories of unselfishness—and it was becoming "more" in front of my own eyes. I saw it myself as people surrounded me and spoke of family, love, and the gifts of kindness that they also had experienced. They said the book was timely and much needed.

The response seemed unreal. It must have felt the same way to the young lad. I can imagine him saying, "I left home with just enough for me, and now look at it! Thousands are eating, and baskets of leftovers are gathered." All I could do was think about my personal reality in light of what had just happened.

When I was a child, the giant oak tree at the end of the graveled road in front of Ma Ponk's house was one of the dependable boundaries that defined my world. From her front room window, I would dream of life as far north as Memphis, Tennessee, but Las Vegas was not part of my daydreaming. Nor was New York or countries far beyond the borders of the United States. But I was in the crowd at the right time, and again God took advantage of the day and tapped into my memories for His glory. What God saw from the beginning of time, I was now about to see and experience for myself.

Prior to Las Vegas, I had neither spoken publicly nor considered speaking to audiences as my life's work. I was determined to build on my education in banking or to make my mark in private industry. Those were my plans. God obviously had different ones, and that morning in Las Vegas He laid the foundation for new directions for my life. What I thought to be a publishing fluke and a one-time speaking event had my future attached.

I could sense something was taking shape, but I had no clue as to what it would be.

Fragments From His Touch...
Life Lessons to Pass along

God will do whatever He needs to do to accomplish His purpose in our lives. In His due season, if we faint not, we will see that multiple roads exist beyond our view, roads that He will use to fulfill His divine plans. And when we honestly surrender to His involvement in our journey, He will lend His presence to our endeavors, making all the difference in the world.

Chapter 3

PHIL DONAHUE... NEW YORK CITY

The response in Las Vegas staggered the minds of my publishers. They talked about it for months. My wife and I were in a daze as well, but we still were not aware of where all this could lead. I could not have imagined the applause and accolades when I lived in my great-aunt's small house in Glen Allan, Mississippi, and when the unselfish living of gracious people were just my private memories. I was content to enjoy this one moment of acclaim for the rest of my life as I went back to the world of corporate America.

However, while I was prepared to sink slowly back into obscurity, plans were being made in New York that put in place another part of God's plan. When my publishers got the word that I was being requested to be a guest on the "Phil Donahue Talk Show," we were amazed. So we began waiting to get the cancel notification. Fortunately it never came, and I was indeed scheduled to be a guest on the

"Phil Donahue Talk Show" in New York City. I was scared. My publishers were dazed. God had to be the only One not taken by surprise.

>When God gets involved, you are often left with your eyes bugging out of your head. You see great things taking place over which you had no involvement at all. The lad brought the lunch, but with the miracle of God's touch, he was no longer involved. He had done his job. He gave to Jesus what He had requested, and the rest was left to the touch of the Master's hand.

>No one—and I mean no one—dreamed that I'd write a book that would have such impact. It wasn't a big book. It really was a small lunch. As I said before, it was not **War and Peace**. However, as it left my hands to the heart of God, the small, easy-to-carry volume was beginning to represent more than I had originally thought. I wonder if the lad from the Bible ever got over the miracle to enjoy the blessing. He probably stood with bugged-out eyes watching his lunch get bigger and bigger and bigger, all the while saying to himself, "It was only my small lunch."

In the honesty and sincerity of my writing, God was laying the foundation for much bigger plans with implications far beyond my imagination. As I wrote stories, God was structuring a conversation for my life, one that was still off in the distance but that He knew to be needed and necessary. In asking for my memories, God took me home, back to the place where His presence was desperately needed to live from day to day. He would pull from that world the unselfishness of heart that would be needed today. Only He knew that within my segregated world, His grace had been present and had been its benefactor.

As He took me home, I had to honestly face a world where I was not welcomed or expected to achieve any degree of greatness. I was "colored" in a "white" Southern world. The social restrictions that existed to separate the races were etched in our minds. Long before I had been born, or my parents or their parents before them, color was used to define and limit social interaction. As African-Americans, we were told where we could eat and where we could go to school. Many of the public places were off limits to us. I recall never being able to go inside the small park that was in the middle of our community's downtown. It was inviting, but I could only look. The large evergreen trees that framed the park were especially beautiful, but I was never able to admire them up close. Though some people were civil within the context of our restricted world, there were those who sought to belittle us in ways that spoke loud and clear to "place."

Yet, it was from that world that memories would be required. Now an adult and years and miles removed, God would show me the strength of leadership that had protected my life and the lives of so many others. Many of our elders became extraordinary leaders in shielding me from the harshness of the system and instilling value in my life through their continual dosages of unselfishness. I was thankful for their incredible acts of kindness, but again, I was only on the outside edges of what God really had in mind.

In 1964, He asked me to write. He never told me His reasons. He just nudged my heart to write. I was kidded by some of my friends in the military and thankfully encouraged by others. When all my short stories were rejected, I became very frustrated. I wanted to quit, but God kept invading my night with scenes from my childhood, so I reluctantly kept writing. Now in the 21st century, as I write these pages, I can tell you that I never dreamed that those cold nights of writing in a faded Air Force barracks would amount to anything. I faced days, months, and years of disappointments, but my heart never quite writing. Thank God, He kept what I had trusted to Him. And He'll do the same for you.

Looking back through God's eyes, I saw what I had taken for granted and others had overlooked—ordinary people who were used by Him to become the parables of unselfishness that He would later grow into a book that would become larger than life. To show you His faithfulness, let me jump just a little bit ahead of my story. The book that I didn't want to write and the one that was small enough to hold in the palm of your hands became a gift to a great human being. I still marvel at how it traveled from Glen Allan, Mississippi, to South Africa. The United States government included my memories in the gift package to released prisoner Nelson Mandela, now the former President of South Africa, a country trapped by a racial conflict not unlike the world I knew as a child.

Once Upon a Time When We Were Colored was in God's hands. I saw this clearly while in Las Vegas, and more would be revealed as the journey of blessings continued. I was being recognized as a writer, but I would learn years later that God's unfolding was just that, unfolding in time. As a result of a plan I was yet to understand, I, a first-time author, was invited to be a guest on the "Phil Donahue Talk Show," the "Oprah" show of my day. This invitation was scary, daunting, and exhilarating. I had never been to New York, and my small book never looked as small as it did the day I received the invitation to appear on the top-rated talk show in the world.

Months had passed since Las Vegas, and with the passing of time it's so easy to forget or overlook the ways of God or to count His blessings as mere happenstance. I had gotten over the publication of the book. It had happened. Along the way, the accolades had made it seem normal. The Las Vegas trip where I surely saw and felt His presence was in the past. No longer mesmerized by the applauding crowd, I thought maybe the response in Vegas was just a fluke. Then came New York and with it the same fear and excitement that I had known when my book was signed for publication.

It still amazes me how easy it is not to build on what God has done. The Scriptures clearly remind us of the value of not forgetting all His benefits, all that He has done. As we remember and voice our thankfulness, we also position ourselves to be ready to embrace the next level of His plan for our lives. Instead, I was as afraid as if Las Vegas had never happened.

As I contemplated my very first trip to New York City, I was reminded of conversations heard years earlier when I was younger and at home with my Ma Ponk. I never quite understood her constant conversations about trusting God and believing that He was looking out for our future. We were still picking cotton and the sun was still hot, but the fervor of her conversation never waned. Now, decades later, I do understand. And it was during the journey of the book that my understanding increased.

When Little Became Much

Looking back over the years since I became a writer, I can honestly say that I see His hand through it all. And I am still seeing more of Him and His plan revealed each day of my life. I don't know why, but He still never gives me the full picture; just a little here and a little there, and then nothing.

I remember one time while at a book signing in Cincinnati, Ohio, I was called to task by a radio listener on the choice of title for my book. You see, the term *colored* had dropped off the face of the literary earth, and I had revived it. After explaining to the radio caller that I was not trying to revive days of legal segregation and forced field-work, but only to capture a time period that we all recalled, I was on my way with a title that caught the attention of the national media.

God was in the choice. I know that now. It just so happened that somebody else brought it to my attention. I was in our upstairs bedroom with my young son Marshall, reading to him from the manuscript, when without even thinking I causally said, "Once upon a time when we were colored." Within seconds lights went on, bells sounded, and I was on the phone to my publishers. The media said it was sheer genius for me to choose to use the word *colored* in my title. The term had been absent from good literature for more than 30 years. I now know the choice of title to have been inspired. The choice of using *colored* in the title was indeed genius. But the genius was not mine.

That's right, the genius was not mine. The young lad did indeed bring his lunch, but when it became a cafeteria for thousands, it is obvious that he was not the genius behind the miracle.

God knew what was needed to catch the attention of the media. Had I chosen another title, my small book may have remained five loaves of bread and two small fishes.

In God's hands, the word *colored* no longer spoke to racism and back-breaking labor; rather, it clearly defined the generation of survivors, the people who through their faith built community in the face of all they had to endure. The people I recalled looked out for others on a regular basis, lifting their sights beyond their divided world. Who would know that during the 21st century, a time of unprecedented advance in technology, parables of unselfishness would still be needed? My memories recorded such a time—a time when lives were protected and nourished by faithful and caring people who were not ashamed of their faith and sought to live it out in our presence on a daily basis.

At night, so long ago, when I was just a young man in the Air Force writing my stories for the very first time, I still recall how they made me feel. I felt so good, all warm inside. I would laugh and even cry as the night gave way to the days in the Delta and I was again in the presence of the good people who had cared for my life.

Now the Mississippi boy from the small front room and the Army cot that served as a bed was headed to New York City. I never imagined New York as a place that would call for my appearance, just as becoming a recognized writer was not one of my dreams. Just going to the library, where maybe these seeds could have been planted, had been denied me. Now libraries around the world welcome my words. I know that this exciting reality has been made possible by God, who simply asked for my small lunch.

I survived La Guardia Airport and nervously awaited the next day when I would be facing a great portion of the world. The next morning as I was being driven to the television studios, I sat quietly in the back of the long black limousine that was taking me through more traffic than I had ever seen. While crunched in the backseat of a New York limo, I eased my anxiety as I had always done, finding in my mind the world of my youth, my family, and my friends from back home in the Mississippi Delta. Thinking about Glen Allan brought the smells and voices of the Delta into the car with me as I remembered the world that had become my stories and the people who had shown me God's heart.

Soon my daydreaming was all that mattered. While we maneuvered through the traffic jams, I was back home almost two and a half decades earlier standing on Ma Ponk's front porch getting ready to leave after 12 years of being under her care. Her house became my home.

And so it is with our Lord. When He takes us in, we no longer have to wonder where we will live or where home will be. I experienced my great-aunt's commitment and unselfishness. They were indeed the steadfast acts of kindness that I needed and that are still needed today. She was faithful, sharing her life and her goods to see that all went well with me. She was intentional, and we must be as well.

Then, as we continued our drive through Manhattan, it was 1965 and I was a young soldier in the United States Air Force. There, of all places, I began writing and actually finding comfort in the memories that were flooding the pages of my mind. It was as if I was writing letters and could hardly wait to finish one and start another. Now I know that God was using all He had carefully orchestrated in my life to fulfill His plan for me.

What seemed simple and unimportant at the time of my youth, like sharing a letter-writing ritual on a Saturday morning, became an incredible tool in the hand of God for my life. In Bangor, Maine, the spirit of those Saturday mornings overshadowed me as I wrote and laughed out loud to myself and silently cried as I remembered. God used my great-aunt's love of people and that of letter writing to set within me the power of the written word to impact and transform people. For Ma Ponk, people were a treasure and keeping in touch with them was essential. I experienced all this in her small front room years earlier, not knowing that God was using her unselfishness to pack my lunch of memories—memories that had now brought me to New York City.

The comfort of the limo ride would end, as well as my private journey back to the Delta and Dow Air Force Base, with me parked in front of the Manhattan studios. I was where I should be, but I was still scared and unsure of all that would take place. I was without a publicist or anyone to run interference for me.

It's so easy when everything is all laid out, you know the plan, and people are fussing over you, making sure that every little detail is worked out. Well, it wasn't like that for me at all. Instead I learned that God and His Word are the same. Scriptures say He is a very present help—and God showed up. When He does, our ability to claim credit for the outcome goes out the window. No publicist on earth can give me a "high five" and say, "I did it for you." I can't give myself a high-five and say, "Clifton, you made it happen." I was scared with no one present to sort out my day. Yet, my day ended up more complete than any publicist could have ever arranged. The glory goes to God. He and He alone did it.

The other guests on the show seemed so sophisticated with publicists all over them, running here and there, getting water, and applying makeup while I quietly sat and took it all in. As I glanced at their books, all much bigger than my own, I began to feel so out of place. Surrounded by this level of sophistication, a story about ordinary people from Glen Allan, Mississippi, was making little or no sense to me as I listened to their conversations about being jet pilots and highly recognized football players. I even wondered if my story would become the butt of jokes. What were my ordinary people doing on Broadway? Would Mr. Donahue honor them as I did, or would they become simple sharecroppers and nothing more? My mind was abuzz with the possibilities of failure.

It's not always an easy thing to trust in God and lean not to our own understanding, but it's always the best thing to do.

I felt so alone in the "green room." I was too nervous to eat the "green" dip and too afraid to go to the restroom. While everyone else laughed and talked, I sat and waited my instructions. So when we were ushered onto the set, it really, really soaked in that much of the known world would be watching. I felt I was up for major embarrassment worldwide. I could only follow orders and watch as the publicists for the other guests took front-row seats and positioned themselves to give their smiles, two thumbs up, and looks of approval to their clients. No one was on the front row for me.

While my head was filled with thoughts of being over-looked or given no time at all, His plan began to unfold in my presence. Instead of being last as I had imagined, I was the first to be interviewed. And even though Mr. Donahue moved on to the others, for whatever reasons, he always came back to my book, even when talking to the other guests about their books' contents. I could not believe my ears or my eyes and quite frankly nor could the frustrated publicists who were up front and close watching all their efforts pale in the presence of a PR God.

Mr. Donahue became caught up in the story of these unselfish lives just as God knew he would. He kept read-ing from my book and walking and talking with the audi-ence. He kept saying over and over, referring to Ma Ponk, "Who is this lady?" "Who are these people?" "Where is this place?" Many of the books written about that time period in the South were filled with the acts of racism and intimi-dation that haunted our lives. Mr. Donahue was aware of those stories, but that day he found himself immersed in another story about the same people. He was caught up in the unselfishness and compassion that I had experienced. Even though the times were bad, good people populated my life, and I had written their story. It was those stories of intentional unselfishness that caught Mr. Donahue's atten-tion and walked him into a world that survived, and in so doing, limited the reach of legal segregation.

God used Mr. Donahue to share this small cotton community with the world and to set me up for another part of His plan yet to be unfolded. I now realize that my small lunch had been truly touched by the Master's hand. Within the context of my humble upbringing, God had been preparing a feast of "possibilities" for the

35

world. New York was in God's plan, and so was the talk show. In just 30 minutes or less, one unknown boy from Glen Allan, Mississippi, was shared with the entire television world. God is faithful and worthy of our trust! He does show up.

This journey to New York, though exciting and rewarding, was only the beginning of my understanding of my place in God's plan. God was using a little book to accomplish a much bigger project. I didn't know that. In fact, I didn't know what to expect of God. Maybe this was all He planned. He was quiet. But He was still at work.

The stories in the book were expanding beyond the covers. Something was up.

Fragments From His Touch...
Life Lessons to Pass Along

We must trust God to plan our futures and to map out the strategy necessary to bring His divine plans to reality. He often works without consulting us, but He never leaves us unprepared for what He has planned. Even when we feel overwhelmed and out of place, I have learned that He is quietly working for our good. Because He has His own schedule, we think that we have been forgotten or will be overlooked. But He does show up. Often He taps the shoulder of someone we least expect to lift us up. He always wants us to know that He and He alone is the source of our joy. Our feelings of inadequacy provide for His show of His love and His strength.

Chapter 4

THE GOVERNOR'S MANSION...ON THE INSIDE, LOOKING OUT

New York was indeed exciting, and I thought nothing was left to compare—that is, until I was asked to come home to the South, back to Mississippi, and tell my story to many of the people who would have overlooked my presence in their lives. My publishers received an invitation for me to visit and have breakfast with Mississippi's Governor Ray Mabus and his wife Julie. "Nervous" cannot explain how I felt. Being asked to come home is indeed the height of honor. Coming home would not just honor my work, but also plant seeds within my head that God would grow into a new and different phase of His plan for my place.

When Little Became Much

As I prepared for this journey to meet the governor of Mississippi, I recalled with clarity how, when I was growing up, I cherished the field trips to our state's capital of Jackson, Mississippi, where we toured the outside of the governor's mansion...not mindful of the fact that because of who I was and how I looked, I would not be invited in. Ma Ponk badly wanted me to see more than Glen Allan, and so did God. Ma Ponk's hands again became His heart for me. Every year she would scrape up the money—money that I know she needed for something else—to send me on those once-a-year field trips.

I could hardly wait for the day to arrive and the yellow school bus to be running and ready. Mr. Moore, our principal, took great pride in those trips. Even though they were plagued with crippling personal circumstances brought on by the social restrictions of the day, he ignored them for our benefit. We could hardly wait to see the sights that the big kids, who had gone on the field trip years before, had told us about. Our little brown and black faces were pressed to the windows of the bus. We didn't want to miss one thing. Many of the places we really should have seen and experienced were off-limits to us, so those windows—through which we saw most of our grand sights—became our only tour guides.

I would no longer be pressing my face to the windows of a yellow bus because of not being welcomed inside the governor's mansion. God provided me a field trip to make up for all the ones I should have experienced. Life had moved on for me, and I had given little or no thought to being left on the outside looking in, but God's heart was broken each time the bus slowed up and moved on. I forgot. He remem-

bered. He was not getting even by ensuring me an invitation; rather, He was building a plan to bring peace. It's not always an easy thing to become part of His peace-building mission, but it's always the right thing to do.

My road trip home to the Mississippi capital came about as a result of the widespread success of *Once Upon a Time When We Were Colored.* As I carefully fingered the date and time engraved on the invitation, I felt excitement. I was on my way to Jackson, Mississippi. However, on this visit decades later, I was being invited inside. Now, for the first time, I would not have to use my imagination to tour the mansion.

The day finally arrived. I was more than a little nervous as Barbara and I walked up the well-traveled path to the governor's official residence, admiring the flowers and the manicured grass along the way. After I rang the doorbell, we waited for what seemed like an eternity before the massive wooden door slowly opened and we were cleared to come in.

As we entered the grand foyer of this great Southern home steeped in history—some good and some not so kind—who should be the first to welcome us but an older black gentleman, the butler, who looked just like Mr. George Stanley. Mr. Stanley was an older African-American gentleman from back home, a neighbor I'll always remember because of his deep-black color and chiseled features. Back home, they all said Mr. Stanley was a pure African with no traces of European genes to be found in his veins. The butler looked like that, black as the oil of Oklahoma and features as chiseled as those on the faces on Mount Rushmore and, of course, that of our Mr.

George Stanley. Although this man spoke only what was required of him, his demeanor and assuredness spoke volumes. It was as if this was *his* house; after all, he had lived there longer than the current occupants. He led us into a sitting room where the antebellum furniture, heavy drapes, oversized wooden doors, and imposing portraits captured the grace and glory of another South.

In this moment I was being given the opportunity to enjoy what others had once denied me. As my wife and I walked through the house, I wanted to touch the sparkling cut-glass vases and sit in every chair. As I stared at the large framed portraits of white Southerners staring quietly from the walls, I wondered how they would feel to know that I was now here as a guest.

God had invited me in to enjoy up front and close what I as a small child had only imagined from the road. God said that He would open doors that no man could close and close doors that none could open. My wife and I had walked through an open door—one opened by God. I wanted such a door when I was a child, but it was being opened by unseen hands even when I was being turned away.

While I questioned my presence in these lofty and ancient quarters, the governor's wife entered the room. I'll never forget her look—full of welcome, telling us we were in the right place.

Though it took me nearly 30 years to get there, I was indeed in the right place at the right time. So powerful and meaningful was that visit that the memory of being denied is slowly fading away. This is what God does when He restores the years! He replaces the hurt and disappointment, yes, but He does so to further His plan.

The first lady was casually dressed in a short black skirt and white blouse, which put us even more at ease, and as she walked toward us clasping my book to her chest, she spoke of the pride taken in my memories about Glen Allan and my life there. I was awed to hear her speak such words of praise and admiration of my book in her home, a place where, because of the societal constraints of yesterday, we might have been invited in as a domestic worker, but certainly not as guests. As we chatted, the same chiseled-faced butler reappeared, as if out of nowhere, and quietly and expertly escorted us to the equally time-preserved dining room. The table was massive, big enough for a banquet, but today *we* were the guests, not throngs of others, just my wife and me. As we were encouraged to sit, the young governor, Mr. Ray Mabus, soon joined us.

We all sat down together to breakfast, and I especially appreciated the Southern menu. It must never change. We were quietly served cured ham, grits, eggs, toast, real butter, jelly, and of course coffee, all on the best Southern china. As we ate, the Governor pointed out the strength of my great-aunt's kind of living and why we need it more today than ever before. As he recalled stories in my book with attention to detail, calling out names and events as if they were his own, he spoke of the power of community...and I heard it deeply within.

It was at this table that the book took on a different and more universal perspective. While we sat in the quietness of the dining room, our conversation centered on community—-relationships far beyond

Glen Allan, Mississippi. Again, the small lunch had indeed become His very own! It was clear that the lives of the porch people were causing others, including people in high places, to have reflective moments about the power of unselfishness as lived out through ordinary acts of kindness brought to life by people just like us. As I sat and listened in awe and appreciation, I thanked God for the value He had placed on our lives. And now others were being drawn into that world that had so clearly defined my life. Little did I know that warm day in Jackson that God was again at work planting seeds for a new and expansive conversation that I had yet to grasp. I would later look back and see this breakfast as an important pier under His plan for my place.

My small memory, my loaves and my two fishes, now a book, had brought me to the governor's table, another small step in God's big plan.

With each significant conversation with others,
God was expanding my own.

Fragments From His Touch—
Life Lessons to Pass Along

God has placed great value on every life, and His heart grieves when we demean any of His creation. What others overlook and often cast aside becomes a treasure when touched by Him. It's all right not to know the details of God's plan. The testimonies of others become critical reminders that He has always shown up and on time. I call it breaking our alabaster bottles of personal blessings so that others can see and smell His handiwork and be encouraged to hold fast to that which is good. It's always good to know that God is in the neighborhood. We'll reap in our due season if we faint not.

Chapter 5

SPEAKING IN THE ROTUNDA OF THE UNITED STATES CAPITOL

After our trip to Jackson, Mississippi, the excitement of being a writer quieted down once more. Life went back to being normal. I had to go to work, and my wife was taking care of our son. The book was selling well, but the hoopla of travel had waned. *Once Upon a Time When We Were Colored* was at this time just becoming another book. I fell back to my earlier thoughts of this being just a book for my family and a few friends. I had met with the governor of my home state, but no dramatic events followed. It had become just another memory.

God, though, was still working. But He wasn't keeping me posted. In fact, I am not sure at that time if I felt there was anything I expected of Him. I was happy in my profession and looking forward to doing well, making sure that every home and every gym had one or two exercise machines. I was enjoying myself. It was proving to be a good year for the brand of exercise machines I sold, and locally in my home-town of Tulsa, Oklahoma, people still pointed me out. Teachers wanted me to come and speak to their students about the era of segregation. While I was establishing my routine, God's plan was taking another turn—one that He would later use to drive His purpose for my life.

As I followed the natural course of my life, doing the things that I should do to provide for my family and live for Him, God was following His natural course. After such excitement in Jackson, would He be able to trust me with more? Would I become full of myself because of what He had done in my life? God was watching my heart and my actions as He took His time in setting up the next phase of our journey. I had experienced to some degree His blessings, just as the lad with the loaves and the fishes, but I also had to realize that once out of my hands, it truly became His, and He would do with it according to His will.

So in February of 1990 I found myself continuing the journey of God's divine plan for my life. I was being invit-ed not to New York or Jackson, Mississippi, but to the nation's capital. I was on my way to Washington, D.C. as the guest of then United States Senator David Boren of Oklahoma, where I would speak in the Capitol's rotunda. This was too much; it was more than I expected or deserved. I could not grasp the implications of being asked to speak to the leaders of the free world and to important people instrumental in shaping our democracy. Yet, this is exactly what happened.

The day I arrived in the nation's capital, I was introduced to the Senator's assistant, a young lawyer from Tulsa, Oklahoma, named Ken Levitt, who worked feverishly to ensure that everything was in order and that all the points of protocol had been met. Unlike the time when I was a guest on the "Phil Donahue Talk Show," Mr. Levitt was my PR man. Nothing was being left to chance.

Eventually the day to speak finally arrived. Everything was in order, and there was no room for error. I thought the people who worked for Mr. Donahue were thorough and strict, but Senator Boren's staff was far more so. That memorable day as I nervously walked through the historic marble corridors, where history was a way of work and life, I was surrounded by voices of praise from people I did not know or had ever seen. Their voices were validating. "We love your book," well-wishers told me as I walked to the rotunda. "Your characters are so warm and recognizable," they said. "Thank you for bringing us inside your life."

As I nervously walked and nodded, their voices kept filling my head with praise and admiration for the porch people who had nourished my life. The closer I got to the appointed place, I could hear the buzz of people laughing and talking as if all present were old friends. Many of them had never met each other, but they all had read or heard about the book that had been written during the waning days of Viet Nam. Earlier I had learned that Senator Boren had invited Washington's "A" list, the cream of Washington's social and political society, to this event. There was nothing I could do but keep my head up, and I did, remembering all that I had seen and witnessed of the good deeds during difficult times. I knew that in a few short minutes, I would be up front and expected to bring the Mississippi Delta to life.

Standing off to the side in a new blue pin-striped suit, I watched as the rotunda filled up with senators, representatives, high-level government workers, executives from the non-profit sector, educators, and students. When there was literally no room left in the rotunda, I watched Senator Boren walk to the podium, smiling and shaking hands along the way. My knees were weak and my hands sweaty as I held my copy of *Once Upon a Time When We Were Colored* close to my side.

When Senator Boren graciously waved to the crowd, silence fell. Before summoning me to the podium, however, he introduced his colleague, Mississippi Senator Thad Cochran. This was my first time in the presence of a senator from my home state. At first I was apprehensive in his presence. I knew the history of our Southern senators. Senator Cochran, though, turned out to be a Southern gentleman and graciously welcomed me to Washington. As he and Senator Boren traded quips about my state loyalty, the crowd roared with laughter. I was still too scared to laugh, and all too soon, in the midst of the senatorial jokes, Senator Boren waved his hand and again the audience grew quiet.

"Ladies and gentlemen, please join me in welcoming to the nation's Capitol a former Mississippian and now an established Oklahoma writer, Clifton L. Taulbert." The hand clapping was deafening and prolonged. Still trembling and shaking a bit, I started to read from the very first page of the book and talk to the audience:

"It was a beautiful October day in the Mississippi Delta and I had returned home for a visit to see the people who had built my world. I could hardly wait to go from house to house to show and tell them how I was behaving in the city. I would eat at their tables and laugh at their jokes and they in turn would look me over, making sure that I had not gotten too big for my britches. I could hardly wait to visit Uncle Cleve. He always wanted to make sure that I was putting some money into savings and Poppa would be sitting on the front porch as always, smoking his pipe and waiting to greet his great-grandson. I was welcomed home and back to the hearts which remained steadfast."

As I read more and talked about the place where I had experienced multiple dosages of unselfishness on a daily basis, I could tell the audience was with me, feeling the warmth of the care I experienced in the midst of the legally segregated society. They hung on to every word as Glen Allan and her citizens came alive to them. They went to St. Mark Missionary Baptist Church where the old deacons and the church mothers still rocked the Sunday morning away as they lifted their faces and their voices to their God. Nothing much had changed. God was still a Southerner who relished loud singing, hand clapping, and dancing in the spirit. And as I talked with them, I could tell they were at church, many remembering a world that they too had left behind. However, for many, it was perhaps the very first time that they had been invited into the private lives of us descendants of slaves who were born and lived behind segregation's walls.

I closed my speech by reading the last paragraph of the book that placed each of them on the train with me, alone and afraid, heading into the rest of my life. I could tell by their eyes that they were embracing the "colored" porter who had been assigned to watch after me. They heard me as I shared my concerns about just how life would be once I crossed the Mason-Dixon Line. I wondered out loud if living up North would be all that I had dreamed; after all, I was leaving my family behind.

As my voice trailed away and the world I had grown up in became faint, their applause grew. I could see them wiping the tears from their eyes. They had come home with me, and in so doing had experienced the feelings of unselfishness that defied my segregated world. Now a completely new set of folk had been partakers of the loaves and fishes I once thought to have value just for my own personal nourishment.

*In that setting, I watched from the sidelines as God extended the conversation from the governor's office to the capital of the United States. The book was now becoming a backdrop for another conversation, one that was not on my mind when I started writing in the quietness of my barracks in the early mornings of 1965 and 1966. God needed the book to start a dialogue about relationships. Don't let a "time lapse" of 25 years cause you to doubt God. Stick with Him. Stay the course. He has the plan. He **is** the plan.*

I left Washington, D.C. with a renewed sense of possibilities, many of which I had never considered. It was the second time that I had witnessed men and women in tears and involved in thoughtful conversation as I talked about a world long since gone, the world of legal segregation where I also experienced the undeniable love of God. Times were bad during my early youth, but God had placed good people in my path, and in so doing left me with a picture of His touch—one that others would need to see and I would need to remember.

In the midst of all this excitement and accolades, my carefully crafted personal world came crashing down. At this juncture, writing and talking was just something I would fit into my real life. Then my real life changed! I had left banking with high ideals to make my mark in the private industry, but it failed and I found myself jobless, a recognized writer with no visible means to support my family. I was scared, but God was already way ahead of me. He knew that there were still more books to come from His touch and that the fragments left over would be conversations shared around the world. He knew that, but I didn't. I would later understand that God was calling me beyond the book. He had it all under control. I just had to learn to trust Him.

My day in Washington would end, but my journey and conversation would continue and another book would be written, emerging from the stories that once lived in a box under my bed. *The Last Train North* would be nominated for the Pulitzer Prize and would place me among the first African-Americans to win the Mississippi Institute of Arts and Letters Award for Non-Fiction. I would again be welcomed home to Mississippi to hold a conversation and spend time.

I left our capital feeling that my book was simply a door to another conversation.

Fragments From His Touch—
Life Lessons to Pass Along

There are no doors closed to God and no positions beyond His reach. He will bring to pass all that He has promised, even when the promise seems impossible to becoming reality. The time He chooses to manifest His words are in His full control, and if we hold fast to that which He has promised, our lives and the lives of others will be blessed. We should consider ourselves fortunate that God has chosen to bring us into the circle of His plans.

Chapter 6

A PLANTATION CALLED GLEN MARY...DWELLING TOGETHER IN UNITY

The response in Washington left me with an overwhelming sense of "God is involved with this book." Though I had recognition, I was without a real job. As I tried to figure out what to do, I went to the old cardboard box and began to look at some of my leftover short stories. From that endeavor, my second book emerged, a book that further established me as a writer and extended my now much-needed speaking opportunities.

While I worried about the mortgage payments, comparisons of my two books were being made to great literature that spoke toward cultural changes. Now instead of one I had two small books—and many calls to speak to libraries and educational conferences. With each introduction, the small books and their value to society were growing. People from many walks of life were starting to take notice. Even the press had begun to slowly pick up on the emerging concept that one could build community with lessons from the past.

The short stories—the lunch of loaves and fishes—were multiplying in my presence. Requests to speak were coming in, and I was not sure of how to handle all that was happening. Then in the midst of all this, I was asked to return to Mississippi to a plantation called Glen Mary in Natchez, Mississippi, to stay with the owners, eat from their china, and be their guest. This would be a view of community that God wanted me to experience, for He knew what would be required of me as I moved into His plan.

God was still dealing with my personal growth. I still needed His touch in areas of my life. Though I had left the South with few personal stories of encountering racism, I was nevertheless well aware of how divided our two worlds had been. There were those places that had been off-limits to my life, the plantation homes being among them. They were places I saw from the road. Did I consider myself unworthy of being a guest? I was certainly socialized by the broader society to think so. But God had different thoughts about me and for me. God had places for me to go and things to do, all of which would require me to have a real sense of community—relationships experienced and passed along.

My return to Natchez for this memorable experience started out with an engraved invitation to be a guest author at the prestigious Natchez Literary & Film Festival. Barbara and I had been invited not only to participate but also to spend the night in the plantation home of Carolyn Vance Smith, the festival's hostess and founder, and her prominent lawyer husband Marion. Until that time I had never spent a night in the home of a Southern white family—and certainly not one of this historic significance.

Glen Mary had been a working plantation generations earlier and was now the home to Marion Smith, a descendant of the family to whom the country home had belonged. Even though I knew the Smiths and their involvement with the festival, this invitation to stay at their home took me by surprise. I was still living on the outside in many ways, though years had passed by. Even though racial relations have gotten so much better from the days of my youthful growing up, "dwelling together" at each other's home was not an everyday happening.

Much went through my mind as I contemplated our visit. Childhood memories that reminded me of the time when I would never have been considered to be a guest in such a home flooded my mind. We were the caretakers, not invited guests. Also, the word *plantation* was not a word I remembered with great fondness. Although the warmth of the invitation from Carolyn and Marion was unmistakable, I was still not sure of the full reach of our relationship. But they had read the book, *Once Upon a Time When We Were Colored.*

> *I was alone when I started writing the book, which God was smart enough to call short stories. Had God told me it was a book in the making, I might have been overwhelmed and chose not to write. He gave me what I could handle, and I am glad He did.*
>
> *In fact, I was afraid of being sent to Viet Nam, and writing brought me comfort from my fears. Once the*

book was published, though, I had no idea as to who would read it or how they would value it. I tossed it out with little expectations of a great return. The book, however, found hearts and homes far beyond my wildest imagination. In so doing, my life followed suit. I was asked to do things I had never done. I was asked to speak in venues I had not imagined. I was asked to talk about relationships and how to build them. People had gotten all that out of one small book—or had the one small book become the initial start of my life moving into a direction of God's plan? Had it not been for the book, I know I would not have been invited to Glen Mary's Plantation. That's the power of God to take our lives into the directions of His choosing for His glory and for His plan.

On the day of our arrival in Natchez, Carolyn Smith picked us up and drove us out to her home, Glen Mary Plantation. As we drove through the old and winding streets of Natchez, looking at all the old homes and the lovely gardens, we laughed and chatted about the festival, writing, the party guests, and the life that defined this small but beautiful Southern town. It seemed as if we drove forever. Finally, the newly paved road gave way to a gravel road, yet another road that I honestly thought would never end. I am convinced that Southerners created long roads so that they'd have plenty of time to talk, forgive, and get reacquainted while on their way. I did remember those extra long gravel roads that go on and on. The Delta is still filled with them.

Carolyn, sensing my anxiety, politely spoke up as any good Southerner would and assured us that Glen Mary did indeed exist. We laughed, and, sure enough, as we rounded the last bend, giant pecan trees, graceful and tall, formed a welcoming colonnade. There, behind the trees, atop a knoll of sorts, sat this gracious old country home. Up to now the invitation had produced only dreams of what our visit might be; however, the comfortable country house, the massive trees, the pond, the moss, and the shafts of sunlight through the limbs of the trees made everything more than real. As we pulled into the lengthy driveway, I tried to keep those haunting feelings of a bygone era at bay, but they still flooded my mind. The Smiths were white and Barbara and I were "colored." I would have been a servant yesterday, but today I was an honored guest.

Even with the warm reception of Mississippi's governor as memory and the wonderful reception in the nation's capital still a picture in my mind, this trip to Natchez where we were to be guests brought back feelings of "place" that had not been resolved. God knew that I needed a new and different focus for the work that lay before me. Glen Mary was somewhat symbolic of the world that had used our skills for selfish gain and discarded our feelings as if they were of no value. I had to deal with my feelings. I had to forgive. I thought I had, but seeing the old house and knowing what it represented uncovered a reality of spirit that God wanted to deal with. Forgiveness is powerful and is one of the tools God provides to all His children. Forgiveness paints a new and different picture and does not provide room for hording the hurts of yesterday. Did I really believe what I was being called to share? Would my meager lunch be of value to the inhabitants and guests of such a grand house?

Looking out the car window, I hoped that my thoughts and fears could not be heard. Our hosts could not have been more gracious. As Carolyn and Barbara walked ahead, I unloaded the car, taking all the time I could. The sidewalk up to the house appeared to be made of ancient handmade bricks, and if so, I could only imagine whose hands had shaped them. Instead of being angry, I quietly thanked the slaves or their kin who had no doubt made this walk, now being used by one of their own. The walk to the house wasn't long, but it seemed to take me forever. I would have liked to keep on walking, but the house, the veranda, the oversized ferns, and the rocking chairs on either side of the front door ended my walk. I was at Glen Mary, up close and ready to walk in.

The next thing I knew, Carolyn's husband emerged and extended his hand. Standing on the front porch, dressed in a pin-striped summer suit of blue and white, and smiling, Marion Smith, slightly balding and bearing an infectious smile, welcomed us to the interior of a history—one I had previously observed only from a distance. Our handshake, though momentary, seemed to last for hours, marked by a lifetime of memories I would have rather set aside, at least for that evening.

The charm of the Old South permeated Glen Mary, and it felt good as we were ushered into this world behind the shade of large pecan trees. The entry was majestic and filled with history. The Old South was everywhere. You could see and feel it as your feet creaked along the old stained but beautiful plank floors. As we were led to our rooms, lessons of family history were pointed out. Every picture was personalized, and renovation stories were told. Our room was just perfect. The ceiling was taller than that of the first floor of the "colored" Mason Hall back home in

Glen Allan, our only two-story building. The bed was a handsome, canopied four-poster, so tall you'd need a small ladder to crawl into it for the night. I didn't want to touch it, but I knew that if I did, I'd be comfortable. The walls were covered with pictures of Southern whites—relatives, no doubt, who probably would not have approved this state of affairs. I know pictures can't talk or make comments, but those framed faces from another time in history seemed to be conversing with each other, and I could only imagine their thoughts.

While Barbara and I were refreshing for the party, the spacious front rooms and dining rooms were being prepared for an affair I will not soon forget. You could smell the makings of a good time seeping under the doors. The thick walls could not keep out the chatter of servants working and the clatter of china and stemware being removed from breakfronts and china closets. Finally refreshed, we dressed for the evening. We had purposely taken our time, thereby giving a few more guests a chance to arrive. We could hear the greetings, the laughter, the long drawn out, "What a lovely setting you have," as only a Southerner could say it. My head was swimming with names and positions of those who would be arriving. The mayor of Natchez was coming, a former governor, a powerful judge, the president of the local community college system, and the publisher of the local newspaper. They all were coming to Glen Mary, and we were the guests of honor.

Heaven must have been abuzz with laughter and excitement as Barbara and I prepared ourselves to be the guests of honor. This would not have happened or even could have happened in the world I knew as a

*child. However, if I was to become a voice for com-
munity and relationships, I needed such a picture, not
just to be observed from a distance, but to be
observed up close from the inside. Even though I did-
n't understand everything that was happening to me,
I knew that I was being ushered into a room and role
that I had not strategically planned to enter. It was
without doubt the doings of God. For me, my place in
God's plan was being discovered as I went through
my natural routine of living, listening, and obeying as
best I could.*

When Barbara and I finally left the security of our
antique-filled bedroom, we entered the long hall where we
were immediately pulled into greetings and conversation
about my first book, *Once Upon a Time When We Were
Colored*, the subsequent movie, and of course, *The Last
Train North*. I sat along with my wife in this spacious
Southern home surrounded by men and women who were
feasting on the stories that for many years I deemed ordinary and of little value outside of my own life.

Most of the guests had arrived, and we were all ready
for dinner in a setting that the Great Gatsby of F. Scott
Fitzgerald's world would have envied. Highly polished silver was everywhere. Southerners really love silver, and the
more ornate, the better. The place settings included more
little knives and forks than I had ever seen. The tall crystal water glasses wonderfully reflected the light from cut-
glass chandeliers. Careful not to hit against anything, I
walked around and looked at everything. However, it was
the spread of the tables that caught my eye. Every detail
was considered and orders had been given—even the but-

ter pats had been perfectly formed into what looked like miniature magnolias.

The only guest not yet there was the judge, an important woman I could hardly wait to meet. As we talked about books and films, Carolyn assured us that the judge would indeed be arriving shortly. While we continued talking about the movie that had been made from *Once Upon a Time When We Were Colored*, the book that was the source of my invitation and always the main topic of conversation, the doorbell rang.

"The judge is here," Carolyn announced as we all stood to greet this formidable lady of the law. I was for a moment speechless. The judge was black! Her name is Mary Toole. The party was for me and Barbara, and the judge was black! Now, with the judge and her husband present, our host and hostess called us to an elegant dinner.

The food, which appeared as if by magic, was superb, and the small hand-molded biscuits were food for the heavens. While eating more of them than I should have, I remembered Miss Bea Brown from back home in Glen Allan. She was Miss Flora's sister; they lived down by the old railroad track, just east of the white school and across from Daddy Julius's mother, Miss Elsie Ford. Growing up, I thought Miss Bea was the best biscuit cook in the world. She still holds that position in my memory. My aunt used to get so upset at me for eating up her biscuits and embarrassing her. Miss Bea would make dozens of these tiny biscuits that would literally melt in your mouth. That night, at Glen Mary, I discovered them again. Arrayed along this elegant table were small plates filled with even smaller biscuits. I had planned to eat only one, but I know I had eaten eight before guilt set in and I forced myself to stop. After all, there were others at the table to consider.

While I was reliving a childhood memory of butter, flour, and grease—drippings from fried pork melded to perfection—the conversation turned to the eclipse. The young newspaper publisher had brought high-powered telescopic equipment through which we all could view the heavens after dinner. The scene I saw as I stood on the old front porch now covered with well-placed night shadows slowed my walking pace. The guests had gathered in small groups, all talking and occasionally looking up into the sky. Then I saw the young white newspaper publisher flanked by the judge's husband, one old and one young, and yes, one black and one white. The old man, his black face weather-worn and framed by white hair, crouched slightly, with his old hands on his knees, as the young publisher guided his view to the heavens.

The black judge was holding court underneath the limbs of the ancient pecan trees. Barbara, my wife, had struck up a conversation with the publisher's wife, and the rest of us waited our turn to view another world thousands of miles away.

I knew the evening would end and tomorrow would come, but for a while in Natchez we were dwelling together like brethren. As I thought about that night, I was drawn to a psalm that I had heard every Sunday morning as a young boy growing up in Ma Ponk's house: "How good and how pleasant it is for brethren to dwell together in unity."

I remember this scripture being read each Sunday morning on the radio station from Greenville, Mississippi, as my aunt's favorite black religious pro-

gram aired. My great-aunt always listened to the "Taboran Hour" and nodded her head in agreement as the one hundred thirty-third division of Psalms was being read aloud. The scripture itself was never discussed; Ma Ponk would just nod her head and hurry me on to get ready for church. Over time I memorized the words, but I had no thoughts of one day seeing brotherhood from heaven's view. That night in Natchez I observed up close how community could look. I was there in the presence of men and women whom society had separated by race, but whom God had formed from the dust of His earth and, with the same blood, given us life. Everything that God has asked us to be is possible. The evening did end, but not our opportunity to live out what I witnessed at Glen Mary's. We serve the God of possibilities who still asks each of us to give Him what we treasure and to trust our treasure to His touch. Five loaves and two fishes were all the young lad had, but it was all Jesus requested.

But there is more. Shortly before I walked out into the night where I witnessed that marvelous scene of brotherhood, overpowered by the smell and the taste of the delicious biscuits, I slipped into the kitchen to meet and thank the source of such delicacy. Where the others were excited about exploring the heavens, I was still in touch with earth. I wanted to explore the kitchen, from which there emanated a lingering aroma that I could not resist.

As I sheepishly peeked around the kitchen's modern equipment, I finally saw the object of my search, a middle-aged black lady who went about her work as the chef in charge. We stood for seconds, looked at each other, and then smiles broke across our faces. After smiling and thinking words that needed not be spoken aloud, I introduced myself. She just beamed. I eagerly grabbed her copper-colored hands and thanked her for reminding me of a delightful childhood memory. "Your biscuits took me home to a time when my world was small but tasty," I said. "While eating your delicate small biscuits, I was immediately transported to Glen Allan, Mississippi, where cooking was a way of life and biscuits defined good living."

As I started to go on and on, a Southern trait, she interrupted me. "Child, I didn't know you wuz colored 'til I saw your picture in yesterday's paper. I have been preparing for you for days." I just laughed. We both laughed. It was she who had made the big bed and laid out the towels and presided over the wonderful Southern meal. Although she had started out thinking I was white, we were delighted to know that we were both "colored." We talked for a moment or two more, during which time I begged for the recipe for the biscuits. There was no recipe; only her memory of a dash of this and a dash of that sifted with flour, stirred in buttermilk, and ladled with butter, but I wrote the dashes down as a gift to my wife.

It would have been so easy to feel ashamed of her position, but that night I was proud of her. We were both comfortable in our skin. She was proud of my skills, and I was absolutely overwhelmed by hers. In meeting her as the cook of Glen Mary, I saw God's child and embraced my kin. I had to love who I was and embrace those whose lives still reminded me of yesterday. If I was to become all that God was planning for me, then I had to grow up and out from my past, releasing myself and others along the way.

A new picture was being painted. I had a new job—one for which I had no prior training. I was being asked to speak and was paid handsomely for doing so. It was indeed a gift. God manifested the gift early on in Las Vegas, but I thought it was just for the moment, not the start of a lifetime.

From Natchez to worlds beyond the Delta, my life was changing. Additional books were still being pulled from those short stories I had written so long ago while at Dow Air Force Base. In addition to *The Last Train North*, I completed the third book in the trilogy, *Watching Our Crops Come In*. I was slowly understanding why God had asked me to tell Him the stories that warmed my heart. As they warmed my heart, He knew them to be of great value to others as well. With His hands leading my life and nothing to hold me back, God called me to Europe. This was truly more than I had dreamed. My hurt and disappointment over my failure in the business venture was being healed as I followed His lead.

The book has become a rallying point for discussing the issues of our past and our future. His plan was steadily being unfolded.

Fragments From His Touch—
Life Lessons to Pass Along

Dwelling together in unity is indeed a precious ointment. The smell is transforming, and we miss this opportunity all too often. The community God envisions for all of us cannot be built in isolation; nor can it be built successfully when we purposely leave others out. To truly benefit from community, we must be intentional about our actions, not leaving such a valuable way of life to chance.

Chapter 7

BEYOND GREENFIELD... HITLER'S GERMANY

From Natchez, Mississippi's Glen Mary Plantation to more conferences than I care to remember, and now to the church where the Protestant Reformation leader Martin Luther nailed his Ninety-Five Theses, is a long ways from my aunt's small front room, but I was there. I stood on the steps and looked deeply into the ancient doors for the nail print that held the theses that reformed the church. I had not come to Germany as a religious leader or as a recognized historian, but simply as a Southern writer to talk about a small town and the people who became extraordinary builders of community during the height of legal segregation. From the very first nights in my barracks writing and talking with myself as God slowly and gently pulled the stories from my heart to His hands, He was preparing me to follow His lead. I was beginning to understand that God's plans were without boundaries.

> *Ma Ponk, who lives way over there? A silly question, but not if you are a young boy and looking out the front room window across the cotton fields that framed your world. Looking as far as I could see and trying to speculate if life existed way out yonder was my pastime activity. There was little to do in Glen Allan and hardly anywhere to go but uptown. Dreaming of travel was not commonplace. My world was limited, but I am continuing to discover that God's world has no boundaries and that His plan reaches out to all His creation. Germany was not on my road map, but it was obviously on the heart of God. To trust God is not to limit Him. To trust God is to know that we all can bring whatever our loaves and fishes are to Him and in so doing set in motion His plans for our place.*

Flying to Germany was easy. The invitation, though, had the smell of God all over it. Although I had personally never thought of my conversation about my life to have value beyond Mississippi and Tulsa and definitely not beyond America, God was multiplying what I had given Him and was steadily pulling me into a direction, though not of my choosing, still within His plan.

While I was in Tulsa, hundreds of miles from Jackson, Mississippi, unknown to me two educators from Germany were visiting in Mississippi. During their visit to my home state, as the story was told to me, they dropped by one of Jackson's premier independent bookstores and asked for a recommendation of an African-American male writer from the South. "Clifton Taulbert" was the name given them, and within months I received a very cryptic postcard asking for more information. Soon after my reply, I was on my way to Germany—my first trip outside the United States.

This early trip to Germany introduced me to a world unknown to a young boy who grew up in the shadow of racism and legal segregation. I'll always remember my first reception, which I now know to have been a prelude for things in the future. I walked into a school where students had recreated my life. Life-sized drawings of my elders graced the walls, and much to my surprise a facsimile of a Southern front porch was built, the place from which I would talk. I had come prepared to talk about the art of writing and the process of trying to get my book published, but my sponsors wanted another conversation. They asked me to sit on the German-made front porch and talk to them about community and what values I could share from my childhood that would help them understand the importance of unselfishness.

In Europe, acts of kindness that I had considered small and of little significance beyond my life took on a much larger role. When the small book reached their world, its value and meaning had already begun to multiply. A conversation reaching far beyond simple memories that warmed my heart was being pulled from my life. Sitting on their wonderfully crafted front porch to resemble the front of a Southern sharecropper's home, it was as if I had become the great-grandfather that I so greatly admired. Poppa's trips to the city in his temperamental 1949 Buick became lessons in the use of personal time. Ma Ponk's willingness to take me into her home became the lessons on the impact of unselfish behavior. Mother Luella Byrd, the church lady, and her commitment to children of the field workers

*being involved in the arts became the lessons of believ-
ing in the gifts and talents of others. As I talked with
them, a bigger story was being written in my heart and
mind. God had done great things in the Mississippi
Delta, and the world was beginning to take notice. As I
made my way through Europe, God would show me so
much about myself and, most importantly, His view of
me. He used the voices of others and their smiles and
acceptance to validate my life as He knew it to be one
of value. I was His creation, one in which He took great
pride.*

I find it utterly amazing that God would choose to validate not only my life, but also the lives of those I loved in
the country of Germany, a place where my color had been
castigated and the racial superiority of those who were
white and blond raised to the level of a sanctioned way of
life. Germany was the home to Hitler, and I knew how he
felt about people of my color. Yet, in his Germany I would
stand and talk about the power of community.

After leaving Worms, Germany, the seat of the
Protestant Reformation, I was invited to address a group of
international educators in a hunting lodge that had been
built for the German ruler himself. I was to speak in Adolf
Hitler's famed Black Forest. Although Hitler and all he had
done were well-known and documented, I always associated him with the African-American track star Jesse
Owens and how Mr. Owens' success had undermined
Hitler's toxic theory of racial superiority. It never occurred
to me that I'd ever be close to a part of the world that he
had so intimately touched.

The day we drove through Germany's countryside to
Hitler's Black Forest will be a picture always etched in my

mind. I was both excited and scared. Though the times were different, I knew that I was deep inside the Germany that Hitler loved. The war that brought him to the world's stage had long since been over, but I also knew that some people still embraced his teachings about racial superiority. These thoughts kept my mind so occupied that before I knew it, the car was exiting the main highway onto the road that led deep into the forest. I was captivated by the immense stand of trees, which looked like soldiers at attention, ready to march at a moment's notice. Although the forest was dense, the sun's rays filtering through the morning fog found every dewdrop on the lacy leaves of the trees, and it looked as if diamonds were strewn everywhere. When I finally found words to describe the beauty I saw, I was immediately told, "This forest was ordered by Herr Hitler himself." I had no response. I was now deep inside Hitler's personal forest and would soon see his lodge—a massive stone structure that seemed to have grown out of the earth.

Our car was the first to arrive. I took advantage of my time and walked in places where I am sure the Führer himself had walked and conversed with his trusted aides. I peeked in every corner open to me, and I went in and out of the building several times to assure myself that I was really where I was. Hitler's thoughts had reached across the waters and in some ways had been alive in our small hometown. Hitler voiced his vicious opinions loudly on the superiority of the white race. Such vicious comments were designed to shape our concept of ourselves and the concepts that others held of us. And in our lives, we faced those who would tell us that our color made us different and inferior, but in the midst of all that teaching, the hand of God was carefully guiding my life for these times. My growing-up life could best be described by Charles Dickens: "It was indeed the best of times and the worst of times." The best of those times were the people who lifted unselfishness up to God as a living memorial.

The Führer was nowhere in sight. And while the hosts were getting the lodge ready, I was left alone to prepare for my lecture. Where once deadly orders must have been given, I would stand and tell stories of unselfishness from the Mississippi Delta. I would build upon the front porch stories that I had shared with the students and educators in Worms.

I now understand that God protected my heart for His purpose through the people who built community for me. And here I was some 30 or so years later traveling beyond the Mississippi Delta to talk with others about the lessons of life that are still needed to build and sustain community. As I made ready to lecture, I could not help but reflect on the time when, as a little boy, I was present when my elders sought to do their part to tell the world who they really were.

Surrounded by part of the world built and loved by Hitler, I went back to the night my great-aunt took me to hear Deacon Joe Maxey speak about his upcoming trip to a national NAACP conference at a time when our community's gathering for that purpose put all of us in danger. I remember sitting alongside Ma Ponk as she rocked back and forth. Even though it was a political meeting of sorts, God was always invited. And in my small world, they knew just the right songs to get His attention. After the singing was over, I watched as Preacher Hurn rose to his full height, bowed on his knees, and through his stutters talked to God as if He were right in the church with all of us. He laid out everything to God, even the travel route that Deacon Maxey would take. He wanted to make sure that angels of protection were placed on the right roads and highways. He sought divine protection.

Though I was thousands of miles away and many generations later, I was still under the protection and guidance of his honest talk with God. I had a right to be at this lodge. It was necessary that I tell the story of the people who built community when facing odds was their way of life. I was thankful that I was able to recall for my German and American audience all the courageous daily acts that others carried out on my behalf—and to be able to fill Adolf Hitler's hunting lodge with their spirit.

The story that God had stored in my heart and recalled for this time was right at home. I watched as educators from around the world were being transformed in their thoughts about their personal roles in building community. They embraced the lives of my people. As I witnessed the transformation of the spirits of those who had gathered here, it had a settling effect on me. I knew where I was, but even more importantly, God through their voices of acceptance was telling me who I was.

Over the years I would continue my travels to Hitler's Germany. Each time I would have an experience that multiplied the stories into concepts and programs far beyond my own thinking. It was here in Germany that the five loaves and two fishes were multiplied into a concept that would drastically change my life. Prior to coming to Germany, I had delivered what I thought to be a one-time high school graduation speech on the "Eight Gifts," which became the basis for the work I continue to do today:

"Building Community With the Eight Habits of the Heart." This concept of the "Eight Habits"—timeless and universal principles—became the fourth book to emerge from the short stories I had written so long ago. In 1997, *Eight Habits of the Heart* was hailed by *USA TODAY* as their year-end choice of books to enrich our minds and lives. And so it did. God was indeed at work.

During this time period, my new life of speaking was on a fast track. *Once Upon a Time When We Were Colored* had been made into a movie, I was becoming a voice of authority on Southern life prior to integration, and people were clamoring to know about the community I had so richly described. It was all good—that is, until a shadow of death passed over my house and my seven-year-old daughter Anne Kathryn died. For months our family bore incredible pain. I felt as if I could never trust God again. I had no joy in speaking. I felt that life as I knew it was over. And I knew that I'd never write or lecture again.

But life didn't end. God was still in my corner. God will complete the good work that He has started. He still had work for me to do. He still had places for me to go, and we were still to see the blessings from the fragments that resulted from His touch. Several years would pass, and I would again find myself marveling at all He was doing.

It was becoming clear that God was using others to direct my thinking and plans.

Fragments From His Touch—
Life Lessons to Pass Along

Let God take the hurt and pain of your life and create for others a story of hope and redemption. We must value every opportunity that comes our way to break our alabaster bottles of His goodness to us, so that others will know that our God still comes to the neighborhood. In our weakness, we see His strength. When we share our thankfulness in the presence of others, we give them reason to trust.

Chapter 8

SPEAKING IN THE PRESENCE OF JUSTICE

Moving through great pain and sorrow, I found solace standing and speaking about my world of the South. One time in Natchez is never enough. Even though I had been enjoying Germany and all the European nations that surrounded that country, I was delighted to get an invitation to return to Natchez. My memory of Glen Mary and the biscuits that melt in your mouth is always reason to come back to this historical American city where each turn of the corner is into yesterday. So in 1999, when asked to come back to talk to a group of industrialists, leaders of government, and noted American entrepreneurs, I immediately said yes.

This would be a literary visit. I would join with several well-known Southern writers who would lecture on the life and legacy of the American South. Joining me would be Shelby Foote, John Barry, and of course the noted Southern historian Stephen Ambrose. Each of us would be assigned to a particular Southern port where their chartered *Mississippi Delta Queen* would dock. I had been chosen to be the lecturer at the port of Natchez. However, this seemingly innocent literary trip would have implications far beyond the bluffs of Natchez and the long lazy river, the Mississippi, that framed its shores. From Natchez, I would again find myself in the nation's capital, only this time at the historic Library of Congress being introduced by the first female Associate Supreme Court Justice, Sandra Day O'Connor. This is how it all unfolded.

The invitation to be part of this group of authors was quite humbling. And when I reviewed the guest list, my invitation took on an even greater sense of divine intervention. The guests were from around the world, many of them members of the famed "Bohemian Society" from San Francisco that had been established in 1853 by Mark Twain and Jack London. The members of this society represented great wealth and worldwide influence. And of all the great Southern writers from which to choose, I was asked to be one of their authors-in-residence for their educational tour of the South. When asked how I was chosen, I found it difficult to explain. It's always difficult to put God's doing in everyday language. How could Philip explain to the Ethiopian eunuch his sudden appearance? Sometimes it's just enough to know that we know that we know.

Rather than give my lecture on the *Mississippi Delta Queen*, I had been asked to address this group on the grounds of Melrose, a large antebellum mansion in Natchez, Mississippi. Melrose looked much like Linden Plantation, another palatial antebellum home near Glen

Allan where I was raised. Both homes were framed by massive white pillars and great live oak trees, some over 500 years old.

When I arrived at the mansion, I could only stare at the sheer size of the house. It looked more like an ornate government building in Washington, D.C. I was in awe of this majestic home and the history it represented. Once inside this national treasure, I was even more overwhelmed. The furniture that remained spoke of a life of sheer luxury when Natchez was still somewhat of a frontier. Melrose is a home where many Americans and even foreign guests would conjure up dreams of gala balls, expensive lace and crystal, and the scent of magnolia filling the air. For me, however, the air also was filled with ghosts and resounded with the heartbeats of those on whose labor those lavish celebrations depended—the slaves of Melrose.

The world of slavery was undeniable. It was everywhere. Without the labor of those who looked like me, this incredible lifestyle of comfort and ease could not have happened. I had to restrain myself from being angry and wanting to just leave. Behind every beautiful painting and lovely piece of furniture, I could feel the pain and suffering of those whose labor was demanded. It was a world where the "slave" muscles and presence was the technological advance. They made life easy for others. And this is where I was expected to stand tall and tell the story of their near kin, my family from the Mississippi Delta, who were descendants of these very people. I didn't know if I was big enough to pull off such a feat, but God was at Melrose too, for I felt His presence and saw His touch.

81

Now, some 175 years later, I—the great-great-great-grandson of slaves—was being asked to take my place on these grounds and give my perspective on the life of our people who had lived in the South, their kin. I had been invited to lecture on the incredible sense of community that flourished in spite of racism and the restrictions of legal segregation.

I couldn't see any of this during the 17 years these ordinary people simply and consistently cared for my life. At the time I didn't recognize the value of what was being given me; nor did I ever expect their humble gifts to become a powerful book. But they did.

With my personal tour of Melrose over, it was time for me to prepare for my lecture. The guests would be arriving at any moment. As I left the "big house," as these mansions were commonly called, that cool spring morning, I could see the houses that had sheltered the house slaves. I also could see the preserved shanties that were home to those who worked in the fields. As I drew closer to the field slaves' quarters, my heart sank. I looked at the newly whitewashed frame structures and was moved as I thought about the slaves who had lived in them and worked these beautiful grounds so long ago. Though my life had changed drastically since I was growing up in the Delta, for a few moments I could feel the handle of the field hoe in my hands and the nine-foot cotton sack on my back. My life in some ways had not been too different than theirs.

When looking at Melrose, I could only imagine the great disparity that existed between those who sought to master and those they mastered. The enormity of this world of slaves and masters must have transfixed me, for I had fallen far into another time. I know God must have sensed my feelings of historical hurt and pain. From somewhere strength came, and I followed one of the park rangers into the small shelter that had once been a home. The more I saw, the less I felt like talking to the wealthy and the powerful.

Walking through the small dwellings with my guide, I saw computers in the places where wooden cots had once stood and where small tables had held meager helpings of food. I watched as the uniformed park service men and women walked in and out of the house. I wondered how they felt. Keeping tabs on part of our national treasure was their job. But the houses were more than a historical place to me; they had been the homes of my kin, the places where they had lived, loved, and dreamed of freedom. They would have been so crowded. Privacy was nowhere in sight. And when I did glance to the outside, all I could see was the enormous house where space and privacy were paramount. As I walked out into the gentle Southern humidity that was slowly rising, I thought that the slave dwellings looked just like the houses I knew from Wildwood Plantation, a plantation near Glen Allan. The restored slave homes were just like the shotgun houses I had seen all my life. I knew people who had lived in such places. I had eaten at their homes and spent the night in their small frame beds. Maybe visiting Melrose was just history for some, but for me it was somewhat reminiscent of a way of life I knew all too well. Silence was everywhere, except inside of me.

My stories looked even smaller as I realized the magnitude of importance that would be assembled to hear me talk. The sheer size and beauty of Melrose had reminded me of just how meager my world had really been. Standing on these grounds and looking all around, my lunch of five loaves and two fishes seemed not only insufficient, but also totally out of place. In my moment of frustration, I was looking to myself to be the bridge between my world and the world many of them knew. However, God had to remind me that He was God over both worlds and would be the bridge I would need. God was not intimidated by their wealth; nor was He hampered by my feelings.

It all felt too familiar. I left the others behind. The others, all being white, may have sensed my feelings, and they left me to myself. I walked away, not to leave them, but to talk to God. I had to pray. I don't remember ever leaving the scene to specifically pray until this time. Yes, I have always uttered "thank-you" and "show-up" prayers on the run, but this time it was altogether different. I needed to talk with God. And I did.

Walking away from the refurbished slave cabins, I stopped where I felt I belonged, underneath the welcoming branches of a 700-year-old oak tree. I was comfortable under the tree. After all, the tree was but an innocent bystander when life was that of slave and master. The breeze from the tree had served them both, and now it shaded me. While there in the clearing, looking out on hundreds of young moss-covered trees, God focused me on the love and strength that had traveled down through the generations and shown up on my doorstep. While in this quiet place, my mind became clear, and without fanfare or trumpets sounding I knew what had to be done. I just knew what to do. I immediately rounded up the rangers and my friends and sent them on a quick journey to find me eight broken bricks or stones, a gunnysack, and an old rocking chair, and to place them all up front at the place I would lecture. We all moved quickly, and just in time it was all done.

I had asked for His help, and He had come to my rescue. The idea to gather broken stones like crushed lives came from Him. After all, He knew the feeling of rejection as well as the joy of knowing that the "stone rejected" became the cornerstone.

The guests arrived. The once sea of empty white chairs on smoothly cut green grass were no longer empty. Each chair was occupied. They had come prepared to listen. And I had come to talk. They sat quietly waiting for me to welcome them into the small front rooms and to introduce them to the people who at an earlier time had escaped their view. With their full attention, I walked to the rocking chair and began to talk, and as I talked, I pulled broken stones from the gunnysack and held them high.

I began to tell them that these stones, broken and over-looked, were the treasures that had been placed in my life—the "Eight Habits of the Heart" of an unselfish community. I wanted them to know how God used "unselfishness" to shape my life. I began my conversation...

"Overlooked and undervalued, the porch people of the Mississippi Delta left lessons on the value of building community for future generations. To find those lessons, I traveled back and painstakingly sifted through the debris of a forgotten culture and discovered and embraced the unselfishness that had secured my future. For the next few minutes, we will dust, wash, and examine this important history."

I gave them an inside look at a world that had no doubt gone unnoticed, and the shotgun houses of the Mississippi Delta sprang alive as I talked about the life actions that God had allowed me to encounter and to later write down. As these seasoned travelers and knowledgeable people fastened their eyes on me, I pulled broken bricks and stones from the old brown sack, symbolic of the lives to be valued, discussed, and prized as they had become for me. God revealed, as I wrote their story, the true treasure of our good living—men and women who stopped to care and in so doing revealed the heart of God. In the small front room where I grew up, we had no choice other than to rub hands and hearts together, and I offered that same opportunity to these listeners. I watched their faces as my meager meal of chicken wings and leftover rice became the food of greatness when shared with loved ones.

Their response was more than gracious. Their hand-shakes were genuine, and their moist eyes told me that they had been inside the homes and hearts of the people I wrote about. It had been a good morning on the grounds of Melrose; the kin to the slaves had spoken "there" for them. It was now time for me to go home. Or at least that was my thought. However, unknown to me at the time I spoke, one of the guests in the audience was Associate Supreme Court Justice Sandra Day O'Connor! I had shaken her hand, but it was only afterwards that I was made aware of this honored guest. I remembered the lady who stood in line waiting her turn to shake my hand and the very positive comments she made about the stories I had shared. It wasn't until later, however, when one of the guests who had overheard our conversation told me her title.

My small lunch was more than sufficient. It fed the intellect, and by the flow of tears I knew it also fed their souls. I listened to myself talk and was amazed at how God kept pulling life out of those old shotgun houses. Talking to these people was like it was the first time. It was as if the "lunch" had never been shared before that day. It was fresh and more than enough. I would later be asked to bring the fragments to Washington, D.C.

Within hours of our meeting, while relaxing on the *Delta Queen*, Associate Justice Sandra Day O'Connor extended an invitation for me to share breakfast with her and her husband the next morning. I was stunned, but I quickly said yes. Who would have believed that a Supreme Court Justice would be so taken by the story of ordinary African-Americans who became the "Eight Habits of the Heart," that she would use her position and influence to bring me to the nation's capital one more time?

The next morning came quickly; they were already seated when I arrived for breakfast. I sat and listened as the Justice reflected on the stories I had shared under the 700-year-old oak tree, embraced by the shadows of the past. I knew that after breakfast I would be leaving them behind, but for a few moments more I listened as one of the jurists from the highest court in our land validated again for me that the unselfishness I encountered in my life had really mattered then and is even more needed today. The judge assured me that I would see her again in Washington, D.C. I politely thanked her, but I said to myself, "This has been history for me, but it is probably never to happen again." I thought I was at the end of a conversation, but it was one that God was just starting. The conversation at Melrose went on with Justice O'Connor to Washington, D.C.

Several months later I received an invitation to address members of the highest court in the land and guests in the lecture hall of the Library of Congress. I held in my hands a copy of an elegant invitation, one that bore a gold foil seal of the American eagle, and there in bold print I saw my name, Clifton L. Taulbert, as the guest of Associate Supreme Court Justice Sandra Day O'Connor and the Honorable Librarian of the United States of America, James H. Billington. For a few moments, I felt as if it was all a dream.

Surely I was not being invited to speak at such a place and to such a distinguished group of people. But I was, and within a few months of my first conversation with this esteemed Justice, I was in Washington. It all happened so quickly and at a place and time that I had no involvement in choosing. I was just doing my job in Natchez while God was doing His. This trip to the Supreme Court and the Library of Congress will be long remembered. I will never forget the reception and my feeling of awe and wonder as my wife and I were personally escorted through the chambers of the United States Supreme Court prior to the lecture that I would give. Though years have now passed, I still can't believe I was in the highest court in the land.

Leading up to my lecture, I recall walking down long, graceful halls steeped in American history, cherishing each step and knowing in my heart that this was part of a plan that I had neither seen nor comprehended when I was young and working the fields of the Delta. While I worked the fields and benefited from those who took good care of me, God was already in the future, moving me in with my great-aunt, sending me off to St. Louis, and providing me in 1966 with the miracle assignment to the 89th Presidential Wing of the United States Air Force when all I could see was Viet Nam in my picture. God saw this night when He tugged on my heart to start writing stories—my small lunch.

On the evening of the lecture, I walked in with the Justice. After being seated I sat quietly by my wife as Dr. Billington welcomed the distinguished guests and introduced Justice O'Connor, who then would introduce me. With Supreme Court Justices around me, generals from the Pentagon, and leading citizens from throughout Washington, I felt lost. It was like a "first time" all over again. My stories seemed very insignificant as I took inventory of the crowd. Then all too soon I heard the words that signaled my time: "Please welcome my friend, Clifton Taulbert, an American voice."

As had happened in the Capitol rotunda years before, my talk—the same stories, the same lunch—was greeted by thunderous applause as if it had never been delivered before. Ma Ponk, Poppa Jo, Mr. Cleve, Miss Luella Byrd, Mr. Louis Fields, and even the man we called the "ole African" brought the audience to its feet. After the applause had died down, I was surrounded by well-wishers, but one gentleman in particular made the night for me. "Mr. Taulbert," he said, "I want to thank you. We hear a lot of speeches here in Washington, but this may be the first one I've heard that really made me think." Making people think about their personal roles in building community is becoming the theme of my talks. After signing

When Little Became Much

books, I walked out into the night humbled and thankful that God had not overlooked my Delta porch people. He was using their lives in ways I would not have dreamed, even among the Justices of the highest court in our land.

God is building His own business plan
for my life from the stories I wrote.

Fragments From His Touch—
Life Lessons to Pass Along

God sees through the darkness and the fog, and when we follow Him, our path turns out to be much different than we would have planned or dreamed.

Chapter 9

COSTA RICA...
BROTHER CLIFF,
CAN YOU COME?

America has embraced my book and Europe's children are reading my words. I still don't know exactly what's going on, but the calls keep coming and I keep responding. However, all the calls are coming from educators or professional organizations. Though each is different, I have established somewhat of a comfort level. I am enjoying the recognition, even the direction of my conversation as the message of the book keeps getting enlarged. People are listening to my voice. In my personal quiet times, though, I am recognizing that this acceptance is beyond the ordinary. But I am still not sure of where it's all leading to.

People had begun to call me lucky, saying I was always at the right place at the right time. I would laugh and agree, but I knew it wasn't luck. I knew God was in the mix, but I was not sure to what extent. I knew God was making the way, but I wasn't sure of His plan, nor was I eagerly trying to find my place in His plan. I was just flowing with the blessings.

God will get our attention. If we really stop and listen, we'll hear Him as He speaks through others and through His Word. Sometimes we don't hear clearly because we are not prepared to give up our way for His way.

In the midst of all my invitations to speak, I got this call and the caller asked to speak with "Brother Cliff." I knew that this call was not from Washington, the United States Supreme Court, or the Library of Congress. It seemed to have come from out of nowhere. After talking with the Christian brother who called me from San Jose, Costa Rica, I did not respond with great joy at all. I was being considered a missionary. It all took me by surprise. I was a published author. As a Christian, this phone call should have been perceived as my Macedonia call. Instead of wanting to know about *The New York Times* review or the "Phil Donahue Talk Show," he called me "Brother Cliff" and wanted to know about my faith.

Remember the young lad and his lunch. It would have been so easy for him to walk away from God's call. In this call from Costa Rica, God also was calling from a deep place for a special purpose. I had seen my life grow beyond my imagination, and the feeling was good. Even though I knew it was all God, it was like I was trying to say, "I fed 5,000." No, I just brought the lunch. God fed the multitude, and I can't take credit for His doings. "Brother Cliff" would know that it was

*all God, but I wasn't sure I wanted "Brother Cliff" to get
in on the glory.*

Somehow the Association of Christian Lawyers in
Costa Rica had seen the need for my story in their country and made arrangements for me to come and not only
speak and lecture, but also share my faith. In my other
venues, most of my talks had dealt primarily with just the
story of unselfishness, not the faith that undergirded their
lives. I felt uneasy, but I accepted the call. Fairly soon
afterwards, with passport in hand, I headed to the
Spanish-speaking Americas to tell the story of community built and sustained by men and women who stepped up
and knew why and how they should live unselfish lives.

This trip, however, would be different in so many ways.
It was my "faith" that attracted their attention to the literary story. They had seen me on an international television
program and when they heard me talk about "unselfishness," they assumed that I was also a missionary. So they
invited me to talk and share the source of my strength. I
was scared.

I was met at the airport by more ministers than I had
ever seen in one welcoming committee. They were looking
to hear from God, and I was praying that God would show
up because, from my view, all I had was a book about
Mississippi. The response in Hitler's Germany had expanded my conversation, but not to this extent. I knew that there
are Christian lawyers in America, but I had never seen men
so open with their faith. We prayed at the airport in front of
everybody. I had to close my eyes so that I would not see
and be a witness to my own embarrassment.

*I am beginning to look a lot like Peter here. I know
Jesus, but this is not the time or the place to "fess up."*

Too many important people were standing by and watching. I went through the motions, but I questioned my heart.

I was all ready to speak in the venues of my comfort, in universities and businesses, but God used a lawyer, Brother Jorge Fisher, to facilitate His plan. Although these Christians had many plans I did not know, I was excited about their plan for me to inaugurate the Alex Curling Lecture Series at the National University. I was accustomed to this and looked forward to the venue. It went well, but it was a side trip on the second day to Puerto de Lemon where I had been scheduled to speak at an Anglican church that would set in motion the conversation that continues to this day, finding my place within His plan.

On my second day we were up early, the Fishers and myself packed in a Volkswagen bus with two Spanish-speaking missionaries. After getting gas and food and finding the main highway, I would soon find myself being driven through the magnificent rain forest and up the coast to the old port city that had become home to the descendants of the Africans who first came to this Central American country to help build the railroads. This was the first time I had ever seen a rain forest, a lush garden of foliage, vegetation, and chirping birds. The plants were bigger than any I had ever seen, reminding me of my Aunt Mary Ann's front room back in Mississippi. It seems as if everything reminds me of Mississippi. Aunt Mary Ann had plants growing everywhere and even birds in cages that were supposed to be singers, though I never heard them sing. This "front room" called a "rain forest" provided a living picture of blended colors as well as a symphony that blended the sounds of animals, insects, and birds. It wasn't difficult to think of God in such a surrounding.

Although I was in another country with people I barely knew, I was fortunate that everyone except the two missionaries spoke English when required to do so. Proud of their country, they pointed out its marvels as we rode along that bright, sunlit day. However, as the night awakened from its sleep and began to replace the light, the conversation dwindled. The dark highway, though thousands of miles away from Mississippi, reminded me of old Highway One back home, where nobody liked to drive at night because the darkness was as black as pitch. The people always said my great-grandfather Poppa Joe drove by sheer faith. On the way to Puerto de Lemon, it was no different. Mr. Fisher had to drive by faith. The darkness that suddenly enveloped everything was as thick as the darkness I had seen so long ago on those small one-lane Mississippi roads, and this was far more frightening to me.

It became even more so as we began to experience mechanical difficulties with the van. The lights kept going out and coming back on. As it got darker and as we moved farther into the rain forest of Costa Rica, the problem became greater. I was afraid. Just as we entered the darkest part of the forest, the car's lights went out! Suddenly plunged into complete darkness, I could only imagine that my life would soon end so far from home. I was afraid I would die and no one would ever find me.

At this moment in my life, nothing mattered but God. We have to face such times so that the enemy of our soul gets the message of our faith. I was no longer an internationally recognized writer...I was just one scared boy wishing to be back in Mississippi where I knew the lay of the land. Fortunately, the God of the Delta was also the God of the rain forest.

The curves were long and winding and the off-look was deep and unsettling. I was sweating, but the driver was as calm as Poppa would have been. He kept driving, praying in Spanish, and bending low over the dashboard to keep the faded yellow dividing line in sight. With a constant sinking feeling, I hunched down with him and peered at the line myself—not that it did any good. The driving got slower and the line grew harder to see. But his faith was strong. He kept his eyes on the road, and I kept my eyes on him. Although chirping birds and strange animal sounds are great daytime companions, in the pitch of night they sound entirely different.

I had almost forgotten the quiet missionaries in the van who were unable to speak English and share their worries with me. However, knowing we were in trouble, they had been praying all the time. They prayed in Spanish and then recounted miracles that were interpreted for me— miracles of God's remarkable presence in their lives. They had seen God's hand in very difficult circumstances and were standing firm on His promises. Most of their miracles were unbelievable, but so was the miracle of the Red Sea. Well, we needed such a miracle that night. They expected God to come to their rescue. I was scared, but their faith and surety were becoming my own.

We kept going, and night kept getting darker. Then when it seemed as if there would be no help, suddenly, out of this thick darkness, a big 16-wheeler appeared around the bend with lights everywhere, passed us as if we weren't there, and then without conversation from us slowed down. Honestly, the truck seemed to have appeared out of nowhere. I heard the prayers of thanks rise as the 16-wheeler appeared.

*God promised to be light in darkness, but this was beyond spiritual darkness. He was becoming a **real** light, and I saw Him as such as the 16-wheeler slowed for us to follow without our driver having to honk the horn for help. We then increased our speed from a crawl, attached ourselves to the faint gleam of the truck's taillights, and wouldn't let go. When we made it out alive, it was clear to me that God was not only at St. Mark Missionary Baptist Church in Mississippi. He was also in Central America speaking and answering Spanish.*

With His help, we made it through the dark, dark night. But it was even darker when we arrived at our hotel, a collection of round stone cabins situated on cliffs beside the ocean. From my room, I could hear the breaking of giant waves against the cliffs. I dared not walk to the edge and look over lest the magnetic crashing of the waves cause me to lose my balance. The setting was as exotic as the language and some of the food, but the history of the blacks I encountered turned out to be not all that different from our own. In a country perched on the edge of the Pacific and separated from us by the Gulf of Mexico and the Caribbean Sea, I was to learn that they also had struggled for freedom and equality in a world that had not valued their presence as equals. And now God had sent me to their world to show them the reality of His presence even during difficult times.

After my night of thankful rest, the next day came. It was Sunday morning. We all met in the hotel restaurant where a breakfast of beans and rice was served. We didn't have much time because we would have to drive carefully into the city where we were to speak, and because of our car problems the night before, we didn't want to take any chances. The van was still sick, so Mr. Fisher suggested that we leave with plenty of time to spare. He would be introducing me at the black Anglican church where I would deliver a Sunday morning lecture, not a sermon, about life in the Mississippi Delta. I had no idea that a black Anglican church existed. This would be another first for me.

Fortunately the car got us safely to the church, mainly because we now had the light of the sun. Although Mr. Fisher lived in San Jose, he was originally from Puerto de Lemon and knew where everything was located. Once we found a good place to park, I wanted to sit for a moment and watch the brightly clad people of color making their way to church. The streets were filled with older men and women, but only a scattering of young people. The Anglican church anchored a corner lot, and from our parked Volkswagen I watched as the parishioners filed into this brightly colored one-story building. The old black women, of whom there were many, all wore hats with scarves of lace. A few young people, like children everywhere, laughed and played as they ran in and out of the church.

When we finally entered, I at first thought I was in a Catholic church because of all the vestments and altar pieces. I was awed by the properly dressed black altar boys who seemed perfectly at home in the presence of the black priest—a tall, imposing man who was dressed as if he had just given a blessing in Rome. In the traditional vestments of the Anglican Church, he didn't look like our Elder Thomas at all. Tall and black, his head crowned with a covering of white hair that was matted to his skull, he called the service to order in keeping with a tradition I had not witnessed before.

Long ago this church and its ties to England had been a source of pride for many. But now, near the end of the 20th century, I was to learn that many of the young people wanted a church service more representative of their African roots. I sat, listened, and watched every face as the congregation sat, listened, and watched me in return. Most of the singing was with hymnals. I smiled to myself as I knew my great-aunt would have been dismayed that there was only one Gospel song. As they clapped and sang this lively song, I thought the church had suddenly taken on the look of St. Mark Missionary Baptist Church. I remembered how my aunt disliked singing from hymnals. She always said it was too hard to read and praise God at the same time.

Although the congregation spoke Spanish, a little English, and other dialects I didn't understand, the faces of these people were all familiar to me. They looked like people from Glen Allan and the surrounding small communities. Introduced by Mr. Fisher as a famous American writer, I had been invited to their world to tell them about my journey and where my own journey began. And though everyone looked like a friend, I was still somewhat nervous. These people's lives had been shaped by the ocean, not a small-town Southern lake. Their homes and dreams had been surrounded by mountains, with elevations far surpassing any to be seen in and around Glen Allan.

I knew that I would speak from the center of the church, right in front of their ornate, sacred altar, just as the old missionaries had done years before back home. When being introduced to the priest, I was informed of the protocol regarding where I was to stand and speak. Also,

I was certainly not dressed as elegantly as the priest. It was hot in Puerto de Lemon, and I had chosen to wear a short-sleeved white silk shirt over a pair of good green slacks, just the right "vestments" for talking from the middle of the floor. I liked that location. It placed me within a few feet of the benches where the parishioners quietly sat.

As I stepped in front of the microphone that had been placed there for me, I found it much easier to be there after having experienced His hands the previous night. I feel that God used the previous night's experience to focus my thoughts on Him and about a time and place very different from the world they knew, but so very much like the pain of rejection they too had endured.

I found it hard to believe that God was keeping track of their hurts like He had done with my very own. Though we were separated by oceans and time, I could read their journey on their weary brows. I knew that the evils they had suffered had come from the same source as did those my family endured and protected me from.

After my introduction, I walked to the front. I could feel all eyes on me. I was the American guest, but one who looked like them. I could feel their full brown eyes on me, drawing from me thoughts of a God who had shown up in my life. As I opened my mouth, they began to open their hearts to my words. I told them how God had raised up a family of people to care for me during the era of legal segregation. My story rang true to many of theirs. Our history had so much in common. As they went with me to Miss Florence's house, the lady from New Orleans who owned the small black grocery store, their faces broke out in smiles. Miss Florence, her good cooking, and her great

gravy were not foreign to them. They laughed as I reminded them of memories of their own. I took them to church
and introduced them to the members of the choir and told
then about Aunt Mary Ann, the same Aunt Mary Ann who
had the birds and the plant-filled living room. And when I
talked about Poppa, my great-grandfather, and how he
ruled our lives from the front porch and with his unselfish
caring protected me from the evils of racism that were
prevalent in many of our small communities, they nodded
in agreement. They had experienced both my joy and my
pain. Because of the unselfishness I experienced, my life
was spared from the emotional devastation that could
have been my legacy. I wanted them to know that the
same unselfishness that I experienced was still needed to
ferry their kin across life's challenges.

As I talked about the small front room where I was
taught the value of writing by listening to my great-aunt
read and write her letters out loud, their faces smiled with
a knowing. Apparently they too had lived their lives in
close quarters, where shoulders and hearts had no choice
but to rub together. They understood eating at dusk by the
light of the flickering flames of woodstoves. And when I
described the small cot that was my bed, they laughed out
loud. They knew the cot.

*It amazed me then, as it still does, that God would
pull out of me a story about a small uncomfortable cot
and it would be of value to ears thousands of miles
away. I wanted a big bed. We could not afford a bigger
one, but somehow this small cot would become a
bridge between people who shared a common heritage. The little boy's lunch was not too small, nor was*

my cot, now that it was touched by God. It was provid-
ing warmth and connection between two continents.

My hometown slowly became theirs. I continued to talk, moving closer and closer to the worn but highly polished pews. Now close to the parishioners, my eyes locked on one young black man who seemed to be hanging on every word. It seemed as if I knew him. His eyes and even his face looked familiar. He was seated on the third pew with two little brown girls by his side, and he looked just like my Uncle Hurley from Glen Allan with his velvety black skin, chiseled face, ivory-like teeth, and thick cap of tight black curls covering his head. He was dressed in the tropical style of his country and was probably in his mid- to late-20's. He sat on the edge of his pew, cupping his chin and listening intently to what I was saying. It was as if no one was in the church but the two of us, and we were having the conversation that his soul had longed to hear. Our eyes continued to meet. Even when one of his little girls would move, I would see his hand saying, "Be still." His eyes never left the front of the church, and they were fastened on me.

However, as I talked about the lessons of the porch people of the Delta, I saw a puzzled look on many of my listeners' faces, including this young man's, and I realized that I had better explain not only what but who these lessons were about. After I explained how lessons of unselfishness were embodied daily in the lives of people I had told them about, their faces seemed to say, "Thank you for reminding us of the goodness we have within our lives."

While I continued to talk, I found myself picking out people in the congregation who looked just liked the people I had known all my life in Washington County. I was a first-time visitor to their country, but I had to tell them I had seen them before. Never before had I been so certain of our common African roots as when I looked out on this crowd of Spanish-speaking people who for all practical purposes could have lived just down the road a piece from Ma Ponk and all the rest of my Delta cousins.

In closing, I shared with them how God had used my aunt, great-grandfather, cousins, uncles, and friends' selfless thinking and living to stunt the reach of legal segregation into our young lives. I wanted to leave them with the notion that their own acts of love and care for each other would serve them well and resonate far beyond the place in which those acts first occurred.

The end of my talk marked the close of morning worship. If only I could have spoken fluent Spanish! There was so much more I wanted to tell them about the life and world I knew. This was the closest I had been to such a spectacularly dressed clergyman, whose blessing I wanted and whose hand I wanted to shake as I thanked him for this opportunity to address his parish.

As I quietly waited my turn, I suddenly felt a strong hand on my shoulder. I quickly turned and looked into the eyes of the young man from the third pew. Up close, he looked even more like Uncle Hurley. Before saying a word, he grabbed my hands and held them so tightly I could feel them becoming numb. Over and over again, he kept saying in heavily accented English, "Thank you, man, thank you, man. I like your words. I want to do more with my life. Do you think I can?" I was almost speechless, but I held on to his hands and promised him that he had not been forgotten by God. I wanted to reach inside of me, pull out every good person who had ever touched my life, and leave with him the "faith" that they had shown me—faith that could keep you during your day and change tomorrow. He needed not just my words but also a vision of himself shaped by people who cared and, more importantly, by a God who loved him. We embraced, and I felt the trace of tears as our faces barely touched. I saw in his eyes such a powerful quest. I also could sense and feel a history of opportunity denied, but the story of my growing up and the powerful community I encountered reminded me of the hope that we both could access.

Looking out of the window as we drove back to San Jose, I knew in my heart that I had been in the right place at the right time, not only in Costa Rica, but also while growing up in the Mississippi Delta. The Christian lawyers had overwhelmed me with their obvious love for their God. I had been challenged. Did I harbor embarrassment? I had a testimony. Why was I hesitant to publicly show my love for God? Still pondering those same questions as I made ready to leave Central America, I realized that internal refining was taking place. What God was making was yet to be seen. Of all the conversations I've had, from those early years in Las Vegas when just a few people knew my name to Costa Rica where I had been invited to inaugurate the Alex Curling Lecture Series and to stand for the first time in a black Anglican church, the one in the Anglican church had scared me. I was unsure as to what God was doing with my life. Having grown up in the church, I should have felt right at home, but I felt somewhat uneasy. I was more excited with my invitations from outside of the church.

Whether at an Anglican church or on a college campus, I was witness to my life and the stories that enfolded me becoming bigger and more universal with each talk I gave and each question I answered.

Truly, the lunch of five loaves and two small fishes was becoming "much" once again.

My place in the plan was still unfolding, but I was unsure about the podium and pulpit. What had seemed like simple calls to speak, to share my heart, were all pulling me in a direction of His choosing. I could sense it, but I was not able to fully embrace it or understand it.

When it was good, I knew it. But there always seemed to be something more required of me. Finding your place within His plan can be scary.

Fragments From His Touch—
Life Lessons to Pass Along

Though we may find ourselves reaching out to thousands and even millions in one form or another, our individual journey will always start with personal obedience. God may have plans that far exceed our imagination, but they start with our hearing, our listening, and our response. The activation of His plan for our personal lives requires our "yes." It is truly our "lunch" that He is asking us to bring to Him...what we hold dear and close, no

105

matter how small. Don't let pride of having much or little stand in the way.

Even if we have to travel beyond our comfort zone, God will go to great lengths to show us why saying yes to His will and His way has always been the best choice. When we do, we are blessed and can stand back and see others being fed.

Chapter 10

SCHOLARS AND EDUCATORS

Returning home from Central America, I witnessed the small lunch increasing as other opportunities to talk about community and how to build and sustain it kept coming in. It seemed that over the years since the publishing of *Once Upon a Time When We Were Colored*, new and expanded conversations and more books kept evolving from those stories written so long ago. The book was becoming like a bottomless barrel of oil. From His hands multiple conversations were emerging, as were speaking opportunities, major colleges and universities notwithstanding. I was excited at being recognized and embraced by such universities and colleges. Here I was, Clifton L. Taulbert or Professor Taulbert, not "Brother Cliff." There was something about being called "Brother Cliff" that scared me. As I write this book, I now know that God was talking, but I wasn't listening very closely.

Is it possible to forget our source of strength? Is it possible to be excited about the blessings of His presence, but not excited about being one of them? Somehow, I now think as I write this book that God was using the call from Costa Rica to check out my denial factor. I was recognizing His blessings but not embracing my walk into my place in His plan.

When I was young, a college education was a monumental accomplishment. Attending a prestigious American college or university was not something that happened as a matter of course. In Glen Allan, as it was in the early days of Costa Rica, labor was on the minds of those in power. College, however, was still a conversation that made its way to the fields and farms. And for me, I would find myself surrounded by people without power, but filled with optimism and hope.

Hope and optimism is a conversation that must be heard over and over again. Hope and optimism must be actions that we see lived out in our presence. They become the artists that paint over the old picture and create a new one that has our dreams at the center. My conversations were now causing others to think about their role in becoming these lessons for the benefit of others. And what better place than academic environments to share the stories of community being built and the long-range benefits of doing so? While I was sitting up late at night on Dow Air Force Base, I had no idea that these simple short stories would one day become powerful reminders of what is required to build and sustain community in this century of incredible technological advancement.

As a young child, I had not heard of Harvard University. It would be some time before I fully understood the role that this great institution of learning had played in the growth of America. However, by the time my book was published, I knew all about Harvard University and Cambridge, Massachusetts. It was truly a place of prestige—one that I admired from a distance. The people who reared me during those days of legal segregation never spoke of Harvard. From them I embraced the black colleges of the South, and for our small town, no college was known as well as Alcorn College. My great-aunt's son Sidney was a graduate of Alcorn, and therefore I would be provided the opportunity to not only visit a college campus, but also be supplied with more books than I wanted to read.

I am still amazed at how I ended up at the right house, a home where reading and writing were prized and getting an education was a must. I could very easily have lost my way during those early years of my life. My unplanned birth was such a burden and after my loving great-grandmother died, my future was up for grabs. Somehow a "way" was made and, as I said earlier, Ma Ponk took me in. By her so doing, I was exposed to an environment that God would later use to direct the course of my life. He was there all along, even when I was too young to recognize His presence. He showed up as hot meals and a cot that was all mine.

For me or for any of my young peers to visit a college campus would be a treat not soon forgotten. I needed such an experience, and God arranged for it to happen. Again, my aunt and her unselfishness were used by God on my behalf. My aunt had to work hard to put her son Sidney through Alcorn College where he eventually graduated and went on further to earn his doctorate. The story, though, is of the trip God used to seed my life for a future yet to unfold.

Prior to my aunt's son graduating, he and his wife would deliver their first child, and I would go along with his mother to the campus where I was provided a view that would forever stay with me. God placed me in the right spot, and I am glad He did. While at Alcorn, I had the run of the grounds—from tennis courts to baseball fields. I was so taken with tennis. I had never seen the game before; only basketball and baseball were played in Glen Allan. I would sit for hours watching the players serve back and forth and back and forth, all neatly dressed in white. I remember all their friends coming over to meet us. God was painting a bigger picture of my universe. College was now not so far off. The visit was at a crucial time during my maturation process. It interrupted the work within the fields and showed me people whose futures were being decided not by their muscles alone. Had I not been placed under my great-aunt's care, this picture would not be part of my memory. College was in my future, and I was getting a glimpse of the road I would one day travel, not only as a student, but also as a guest lecturer.

Long returned from Costa Rica, I still found myself responding to requests to return to Europe where I worked with many of the educators who taught for the Department of Defense. Again the source of my information flowed from the same small book that Phil Donahue wondered out loud about the people and their unselfishness. Phil Donahue saw an incredible community within the pages he read, and so had many of the educators in Europe. After spending time at embassies and Department of Defense schools off and on for several years, I was asked to lead a leadership forum in the United States for a number of the Department of Defense educators. This particular forum was filmed by C-Span and shown all over the C-Span world. Again the same stories about the same people from the same town were multiplying in front of my eyes.

I had never thought of being a consultant to educators and certainly not to those who educated internationally. Yet, it was happening. Seemingly from out of nowhere, I was being hailed as an expert on the issues of community. The people from Glen Allan had taken on a larger-than-life role. They were teaching, lecturing, and holding significant forums of understanding around the world, yet for the most part had never left Glen Allan. All I can say is that I am walking in a direction that feels comfortable and good things are happening along the way. Crowds beyond my view were feasting from small stories that had now become big conversations.

With my conversation on community being shown on C-Span, even more calls began to come, and they all wanted to talk about the application of my concepts to their profession. By this time my stories had become concepts. Also around this time I received a call that I never anticipated. I was asked to be a guest professor at Harvard University's Principal's Center. I had no portfolio of strategic initiatives for educators. All I had were the same people from the same town who had raised me. Their unselfishness was in demand, and I was being asked to deliver their conversations, now called strategic initiatives.

In 1965 when I started writing, I didn't see any of this. I had no idea that any of the incidents that happened were in my future. Just getting the book published was more than I ever dreamed. I didn't have thoughts of its international acceptance. I just wanted my family to embrace it—and, of course, a few friends. But it was God's doings. I know that now. It is so clear that all things work together for good for those who are called according to His purpose. Going to Harvard was strictly His idea. I was not bold enough to have dreamed that big.

The summer day finally came when I found myself in Cambridge, and I must say it was all that I had imagined and more. It was intimidating, but in a good way. To say the campus took my breath away is an understatement. No one could know how exhilarating this opportunity was for me. I had been asked to lead one of several leadership discussions for an international gathering of educators, secondary principals from around the world and within the United States. In one setting, my porch people's life became a leadership lecture to representatives from throughout the world.

From the ice house in Glen Allan to the pool hall uptown, these educators were invited to think about the consequences of unselfishness in situations not necessarily of our choosing. These wonderful people and their simple yet powerful way of living had meaning for these times. We talked extensively about the value of time and how to best use it. The example I used was that of my great-grandfather Poppa Joe and our infrequent, but fun-filled trips on Saturday to Greenville, Mississippi, the queen city of the Delta. In that simple story pulled from my memory in the 1960's, educators some 30 years later learned from Poppa's action that if you really want to build a good community, you have to have time for people. This lesson had value for them as they contemplated their relationships with students, peers, and families. Technology often sends a different message about time, but Poppa sent one that was timeless.

The audience listened, took notes, and applauded. They also stood on the front porch with my great-aunt each morning to pull the light string so that the bus driver would know that I was going to school. I told them that she never missed a day for the four years I attended school in Greenville. Her life was appreciated and became for many of them a template by which they could build community into classrooms that I would never see, all around the globe. So much was coming from such a small place, and it seemed as if the more I gave out, the more was left to share. They all responded, and many of them called for me to come to their schools and share these lessons with their parents and teachers. Though my elders looked the same, their conversation, now touched by God, was reaching far beyond the front porches and fields where they were the life lessons I witnessed.

For many people, this all may be commonplace and of no great consequence, but not for me. I still marvel. I know from where I came and the limitations that abounded. To think that, even while I was picking cotton, God was thinking of me and the day He would allow me to stand and lecture as a guest professor at Harvard. Harvard is the oldest university in the United States. As such, it sits at the pinnacle of American academic institutions and is the university against which all others appear to be measured. Being at Harvard was more than a dream come true. It showed me the reach of God's touch.

However, my invitation to Talledega College showed me the depth of the well from which the "unselfishness" I had encountered was drawn. At this small African-American college, I again saw the faithfulness of God in an unlikely place at an unlikely time. Being at Talledega College was a lesson I needed to experience. I was invited to lecture, but the story of the campus lectured me.

When I first arrived on campus, I experienced a great rush of memories from my youthful visit to Alcorn College, now Alcorn University, even though that trip had been some 40 years before. I knew I was at the right place and that the invitation had come at the right time.

Although some of the students and faculty had read *Once Upon a Time When We Were Colored*, they wanted me to tell them more, and I was honored to be able to do so. These young people were painfully aware of justice denied and the condition of life that I knew so well, but I also had a chance to tell them about the strength and the hope that had been protected and nourished within my heart. The students were young and filled with passion for justice and equality in a world that had denied them many of the benefits freely given to others. Many of them were filled with anger at how the country had continued to fall short of those ideals, but many had not experienced the close-knit relationships that maneuvered my generation through tumultuous times. Where I lived and grew up had prepared me for this conversation.

I remember when my military friend, Paul Demuniz, read my first short story and encouraged me to continue my pursuit of writing, I timidly envi-

sioned a magazine buying one or two. Never in my wildest dreams did I imagine being on a college campus reliving my youth. Five loaves of bread and two small fishes were just what I needed. I had been sustained by the kindness that had surrounded my life. However, each small memory that became a small story was laid in His hands, and from His hands generations not yet born would eat. Paul became God's mouthpiece for me to continue my writing. Through Paul's voice, I found the encouragement I needed to write what needed to be said decades later. I thought banking would be my career—and so did others. But God's plan was already in process.

As the packed auditorium listened to my words, I told them about how my great-aunt, a single mother, not only raised expectations for her own boys but also extended those dreams through others, like me, who would come to live at her house. I wanted them to hear the stories of the unselfishness that broke the strength of legal segregation and racism. They had to understand that fieldwork did not define our lives. Eyes toward the future were always there, even in the cotton fields as the older people and their faith kept us believing in a day of refreshing that would surely come.

They were young and ready for the world to receive them as equals, and rightly so. So I had to make sure that they understood that I was not trying to take them back to a world of subjugation but to a place in time where well-placed faith had held hands and hearts together. I had been there to see it happen. They were quiet and attentive as I walked them back to Poppa Joe's and Mama Pearl's big house, where I as a young lad had sat with the elders as they patiently waited for Mama Pearl to draw her last breath. So committed to each other were they that no one was allowed to die alone. From watching them, I knew what would be required of me. As I talked and they listened, they were with me in all the places and among all the people whose lives had nurtured my own for such a time as this.

The lecture was over, but the applause went with me as I was led from the auditorium to have the mandatory tour of the campus. As we walked in the heat of Alabama, I smartly chose to walk close to the trees that provided some degree of shade from the sun. In the midst of my tour, the host said, "You must see Swain Hall." It wasn't far, and I could see this beautiful before-the-turn-of-the-century building. Southern pillars always stood out to me as the best of architectural design.

While I admired the building as we walked up the stairs, the story I heard became the lesson I needed to touch and feel. When we walked into the building, with great pride my host told me the story of newly freed slaves who were instrumental in the purchase of this building and property. With the stench of slavery still in the air, they were being moved by unselfishness. They were looking out for students not yet born. I listened to the story of how the newly freed slaves, filled with promise for their future, walked to New Orleans to the Freedman's Bureau, an agency established after the Civil War, and they along with the American Lutheran Church bought back for themselves the building they had built with their own hands. Swain Hall, when built, was not part of their future. Even the graceful and lovely old trees had been planted by freed slaves on Talladega's campus. They probably never had the opportunity to benefit from the shade provided, but their hearts said, "Do it. Your children will need the shade."

*The unselfishness of my porch people—my fami-
ly and neighbors in Glen Allan, many of whom were
descendants of Alabama slaves—drew their
unselfishness from a well that ran deep. Even the historian at Swain Hall was quick to tell me about the
faith of the newly freed slaves. I guess unselfishness
looks the same regardless of the generation in which
it shows up. The newly freed slaves, motivated by
their faith and unselfishness, gave what they had, and
the return on their unselfishness is seen in the faces
and lives of the thousands of students who walk with
heads held high on the same grounds where their
ancestors once toiled. I was beginning to understand
that my story was rooted in a much deeper one.
Something was happening inside me. I was feeling
the pull on my heart as I continued to have new conversations about the same people from the same
place and from the same time.*

*The witness of His presence was all around me, but I
am still not sure how to classify this gift of conversation. By now, even I recognize that the book, though
it looked like any other book, was out of the ordinary.
God was involved, and my conversations were having impact far beyond my expectations. Hearts were
being changed, and I still didn't know exactly what to
do. However, I did know enough to stay the course. I
kept talking about community and relationships.*

Fragments From His Touch—
Life Lessons to Pass Along

With God, all things are possible. I know that now, and I affirm to you that He can be trusted. Look for His lessons in all the places of your life. Don't limit His voice. Be open to His heart.

Chapter 11

IRISH MAYORS AND KENYAN DELEGATES

Where do you go after you leave Harvard? What do you look for after sensing the depth of the well of unselfishness on a small Alabama college? For me the choice became rather easy. I said yes to being a keynote speaker at the International Sister Cities Conference—a conference where delegates and mayors from cities around the world gathered to build relationships and, yes, to build community beyond their artificial borders.

Sitting on my Poppa's front porch as a kid, all I could see were cotton fields and sharecroppers' homes, and I enjoyed their company. When I left them, I took with me all the memories from the porch, all that I had seen and heard. Now these memories that became the book and the conversation that took me to places far beyond my front porch view will stand me before mayors and official delegates from around the world at the Sister Cities International Conference. Of all the strategic topics to be discussed when that many world leaders are together, the conference coordinators wanted me to talk about the "porch people from the Mississippi Delta."

The conversation from the porches of the Delta, though at the time meant for my ears and my growth, had been given to God. It had started so long ago when I was barely 19 and a soldier. Now a path is being laid out for me and a conversation has been constructed, one that is reaching both the powerful and the lowly—all from one small lunch. If I had been asked to plan my future, knowing that it would have included the governor of Mississippi, a speech in Las Vegas, a lecture in Hitler's hunting lodge, or a testimony in a black Anglican church, I would have no doubt wanted to prepare something that spoke to the economy, the challenges of advancing technology, or at least the need for peace in a global society. I have been led to places where all those topics would have been par for the course, but I, instead, talked about the power of simple acts of unselfishness and how those acts protected my life so long ago. And it seems that from my simple memories came "food" for hungry hearts around the world. I didn't have much to give, but I gave all that was given me, and God did the rest.

I would see it all over again at this international conference. I recall walking into the hotel, which truly looked like the world. Tongues were being spoken that no one understood other than the person to whom the conversation was directed. The dress was indeed international. Robes were flowing and turbans were everywhere. It was so international that I felt as if me and my English were out of place. For a few moments I just stood and marveled at all I saw. And then in the midst of my excitement, it dawned on me that this was indeed my audience. I had to speak to these people. Listening to them in the lobby talk about economic issues of great concern and even issues of military conflict, I wanted to pack up and leave. I looked in the program, and my picture was there. My topic was there, and I was not a concurrent speaker. They all would be present.

Can you picture Jesus telling His disciples to "group" the people in small groups to allow for conversation while eating when all He has are five loaves and two fishes? They must have thought Him to be out of sync. I would have. I was now feeling somewhat similarly. My small lunch had already been requested, the protocol for attendance had already been established, and the meal from the Mississippi Delta had to become international on the spot. To say I was nervous is an understatement. How would you have felt if you looked out on a crowd of thousands and you were asked to give your lunch, especially if you had left home not expecting to be an answer to mass hunger? I too had left home not expecting my personal life lessons to be of value to anyone beyond me. God in the midst of the need makes all the difference. And I was to witness it once again.

The day arrived for my speech, and as expected the ballroom was filled to capacity. Because it was a plenary session, the guests were all dressed in their finest, representing their countries in style. From where I sat on the platform, I could look out and see the world. To think that, as a child, all I could see from my great-grandfather's front porch were cotton fields and sharecroppers' homes. Now, decades later, I am sitting down and looking again as far as I can see. After the preliminaries were over, I was graciously introduced. Out of courtesy the audience applauded. Then I stood up and began my speech, their journey to Poppa's house.

After I explained the backdrop of legal segregation and the presence of racism, they also began to understand the power of unselfishness as timeless and necessary for any people at any time. It seemed as if "selfishness" looked the same all over the world. Feeling "ignored and looked down upon" caused the same feelings of self-doubt no matter the language spoken. It also seemed as if a "kind word" lifted hearts in any language and an act of courage to "better the life of someone else" was not foreign to any of those listening.

As I walked off the stage into the audience, looking into eyes along the way, something universal was happening. People from around the world were eating the same meal and responding as one. I was talking, but God was feeding. His "touch" was being received at a level beyond my understanding. Walking back to the platform, I closed my speech with the story of an old man from my community who was called by all the "ole African." He stuttered as he talked while walking throughout our community admonishing our parents and elders that we, their children, were indeed marked for good. The "ole African" story caused them all to rise to their feet in thunderous applause. The applause came from England, France, Germany, Ireland, Africa, the islands of the seas, and the Americans who were present. Their standing applause validated the fact that people still need each other to tell them that they are of worth and value. One voice can still make a difference.

I was literally mobbed as I made my way to the book signing table. However, along the way I was held up by the mayoral delegation from Kenya. I was honored to be in their presence but not really prepared for what their leader had to say. As we shook hands, hugged, and kissed, their leader, richly and ornately dressed, looked at me and without even flinching an eye said, "Today we have been in the presence of God."

I stopped dead in my tracks. I had not expected such a statement at such a place. I was, after all, an international lecturer, not a preacher. At that moment I thought of the lawyers in Costa Rica who had insisted on calling me "Brother Cliff." How could he say that they felt as if they had been in the presence of God? I too had felt something, but at this point I wasn't ready to call it the presence of God. But I knew that my talk was indeed becoming more than five loaves of bread and two fishes. Truth is being revealed, and I am being perceived as a messenger. I remember walking away quickly from the Kenyan leader, but his words, "Today we have been in the presence of God," stayed with me.

I left the Kenyan delegation unsure of the full meaning of all that I had heard. I just know that it stumped me. I had to think differently for a moment. I certainly wanted my speech to be accepted, but I was not prepared for some to say that they felt the presence of God. What was I really doing, and did I want to go down this road that others were sensing? These questions lodged inside my head and heart as I proceeded to the autographing area where within a few hours, most of the books were gone.

With the book signing over, I thought I was through. I wanted to mingle with the guests, not think about the Kenyans; however, although I may have been through, the meal was still being served. While I made ready to leave the table, I noticed standing across from me a group of men, all sporting big red bushy beards, looking my way. One of the men got my attention, and after closing down the book table I walked over to this group of red-bearded men.

They quickly said that they were from Northern and Southern Ireland. Hearing those two places mentioned together, my mind began to run to the newspapers and the late-night news. These groups should not have been standing together. The men formed a circle, and I found myself in the middle of this group of mayors from Northern and Southern Ireland. I didn't know what to expect, and I was surprised to find myself in the middle of their two worlds. I felt I should not have been in the middle, but it's amazing what a meal of "touched" bread and fish can do for those who are hungry for peace and community. I was blown away. In just a few short hours, I was being a bridge over troubled waters.

After my speech, they all had purchased a copy of my book and were clutching the book in their hands. They had waited to personally talk with me. Not only were they together, from the north and the south of Ireland, but their faces were wet with tears. They had been crying. And there I was, the little boy from Glen Allan, Mississippi, in the midst of a circle of tall, red-headed, red-bearded men with tear-soaked faces clutching copies of my book in their hands. Catholics, Protestants, and me all standing together, all removed from the pain of our lives as we embraced each other. They wanted to know more. Their hearts had been touched! We continued to embrace each other as we recognized our shared humanity and common faith. In some small way, maybe telling my story of struggle and triumphs had quickened their thoughts of reconciliation.

We stood in our circle talking and crying. I know that people were watching us, but I didn't really care. I knew this to be the right thing to do. I never dreamed I would stand in the midst of men whose lives were dogged by such internal conflict, international terrorism, and an ongoing religious civil war, but there I was...welcomed into their group because of the meal of memories they had just experienced.

They heard the story. They knew my place to have been small. They listened to the struggles and bore witness to the acts of kindness that surrounded my life. They were hungry for hope, and the stories they heard fed their souls. It was as if I had prepared my speech just for them. The mayors wanted to talk about the taste of what they had eaten. They wanted to know about the seasoning. Though it may have been different, they liked it and found it to be quite filling. Their hearts were full and their eyes overflowed as this food lifted their sights to a better day. Was God in the Delta decades ago preparing a meal for His Irish children?

As with our own country of America, Ireland over the years had become divided into its own North and South. And within this division, there were the Protestants and the Catholics—both of whom claimed to have the true interests of the people at heart. Ireland's fight with England and the aggressiveness of the IRA had brought this country's battle into our homes in America. And today these mayors were no longer just figures on the evening news but people with whom I was crying and weeping for their hearts' cry to become reality.

I listened as one by one they told me how they had been moved by these stories from the Delta. Personal commitments to unselfish living in spite of legal segregation had caused them to recognize that powerful transformation often starts with simple, unselfish acts. As they spoke, I wished that what I was seeing could have been transported to their country for all to see and understand. In those moments and within our tear-soaked circle, there was no talk of war, bombing, or religious differences, only our shared humanity. I knew that Ireland was still a country divided, but in spite of that, I stood in the midst of political leaders from both sides of the conflict. They all looked liked first cousins to me, innocent boys who had grown up and inherited a war of wills started long ago. For a while we were as one people at one annual meeting with only one major concern—lifting relationships higher than differences. They wanted me to come with them to Ireland. They wanted their people to hear firsthand these stories that had pulled tears from their eyes and challenged their hearts. I listened as they talked, thinking all the while that only God could have gotten so much for so many from such a small place.

As I left their midst, I valued the lives that God had allowed me to experience even more. My parents' generation and the ones before them often faced personal violence, threats to their lives, neglect, and a sense of being without a country. And I could have grown up with that same reality and a life developed from that point of view. However, in the face of my uncertain future, God showed up at my birth and took control of my life, placing me in the right homes and among the right people who would be instrumental in shaping the view I would need for my future.

As my story—one of "faith" lived out and passed along—became bigger than life for all of us, the Irish mayors recognized the power that could come from one person's commitment to daily unselfish living, even if the surrounding circumstances were not the best. I don't know if they saw their "faith" as the source of that commitment, but I tried to leave with them the reality of my own. For a brief moment, the porch people of the Mississippi Delta became the United Nations and potential instruments for peace. And I hope that the lessons of life shared will be food to the hearers as they continue to be for me...sustaining them as they embrace to build their own powerful and fulfilling community. We are continually sustained by the testimonies of those who pass before us.

As you move more into God's plan, you will begin to experience less of yourself and more of Him. You are doing the work, but the increase seems to be more than you remember planting.

**Fragments From His Touch—
Life Lessons to Pass Along**

Simple honesty and sincerity place our life within the lives of others. And from such a vantage point, people can often stand on their tiptoes and see God.

Chapter 12

CHINA'S HONG KONG...BEYOND THE DELTA TURN ROADS

It was becoming quite evident that my small lunch was destined to feed people beyond the borders of my country. I had just witnessed the response of the Kenyan delegation and shared the hugs and tears of the Irish mayors. Now I am on my way to Hong Kong as a keynote speaker for an International Educators' conference on Character Education. After years of being taken for granted, the subject of "character" at the adult and juvenile levels was now becoming a major topic of conversation, not just within the United States, but all over the world. Character development, once considered the sacred domain of homes and places of faith, had moved into the academic arena. Both educators and parents were becoming alarmed at the behavior of some of our young people. As grades and tests scores spiraled downward, the issue of behavior was spiraling upward. Something had to be done; thus the advancing march toward formalizing curriculums and initiatives that could impact student behavior.

It was into this arena of "character education" that the stories from my small community would be invited and become part of the national conversation on the subject. Life that I had witnessed from the safety of my porch people's world was now being perceived by many to have answers to the behavior problems being experienced in many of our schools. I was being invited to bring the "Eight Habits of the Heart" to this international gathering. Over the years, the story of my great-grandfather's unselfishness personalized the habit of "Nurturing Attitude." "Responsibility" had become Mr. Cleve, the local iceman. "Dependability" became Ma Ponk, and her steadfast attention to my life became the look and feel of this habit of the heart. The "Blind Berta" story personalized and further fleshed out the look and feel of the habit I now called "Friendship." My employer, a white lady from my hometown of Glen Allan, became the personalization of the habit known as "Brotherhood" as she included me in her life. And the habit I called "High Expectations" has been introduced around the world as the "stuttering ole African." "Courage" was Fannie Lou Hamer, Jake Ayers, and Ole Miss's Reverend Roy Grisham, all Southerners who sought to live their lives beyond what was socially acceptable and who set out to do the right things. "Hope," the eighth habit of the heart, is my birth mother Mary, who by her unselfish actions became the personification of hope for me and my siblings and countless thousands who were touched by her life. These people from Glen Allan who were being called men and women of character now had an opportunity for their lives to help shape the thinking and the actions of young people far beyond their front yards and front room windows. This conference would leave little doubt that little was becoming much. It was happening before my very eyes. God was talking, but I had yet to listen with my whole heart.

In China's Hong Kong I experienced an incredible acceptance of the people whom I had written about so long ago, wrapped in a military blanket on Dow Air Force Base when I was only 19 years of age. I often wonder what would have happened had I not written the first story. I felt the urging to do so, but I doubted my ability and I had no pressing reason to write. When talking with my military buddies, many of whom had come from major cities, my life seemed even more dull than usual. I had no pressing need to record my story. But I listened to my heart and wrote anyway. And now I am on my way to one of China's well-known provinces, Hong Kong.

China was always talked about in the Delta as the really faraway place. In fact, when I was a kid and too young to work in the fields, I would go along with my aunt and she, to keep me out of trouble, would sit me on the tractor turn road, give me a stick, and tell me to dig my way to China.

Ma Ponk and her friends never anticipated their lives becoming a pattern for responsible living. I never expected my late-night stories to become the basis for a concept of living called the "Eight Habits of the Heart." Glen Allan was that part of the economy that exported cotton to the world, but as you now know and will continue to witness, another valuable export commodity was being made ready at a time when it looked as if nothing good was happening.

When Little Became Much

How do you get from Glen Allan, Mississippi, to Hong Kong, China? You listen closely to your aunt who, upon leaving you on the field turn roads, admonishes you to stay out of trouble by digging your way to China. You'll find that you can't dig your way to the land of silk and spices. It is a remote place, one of which my aunt had no knowledge. She never imagined experiencing such a place. She just knew that her instructions would keep me out of trouble. She would give me my orders, laugh, and walk away. And I would dig and dig. Only God knew that I would one day write my way to China.

Though it was many, many decades later and yes, because of a book that I had written, I finally made it to China. I was invited to China's Hong Kong by Charles W. Dull, Will Chan, and Chuck Steinbach, educators from a rather large private Christian school. When I reached the Hong Kong International School after race-car driving through narrow streets, I was glad to see Will Chan, a tall, distinctive Chinese gentleman. He extended his hand and welcomed me to this ancient harbor where the school was located and where business had been transacted hundreds of years earlier. As we stood and talked, we traveled back to a different time—one of sea-faring merchants and pirates. I was completely taken by the conversation and was a bit sad when it ended; but after all, I had been invited to lecture and to talk about building community and character development. All of which would emerge from the "small memory" that had now become an international conversation. Glen Allan's simple lessons had found their way to this Far East harbor and to these people from around the world.

As I was growing up, God allowed me to witness good relationships being built and good character being molded. Little did I know that those observations would later prove to be powerful relationship-building skills from which good character would emerge. It would be important for this century to understand the dynamics of relationships and how they are built and sustained. I witnessed the timeless answers from my small, front room view. Then, it was just "everyday stuff"; nothing special, just the way things were. Now I know God was in the midst of legal segregation and racism, building relationships in my presence and developing character—a subject that I would later discuss.

Well, I would soon find out that Mr. Chan and Mr. Steinbach had me scheduled to speak that evening to a collection of students, parents, and educators all at one time. I laughed out loud when they informed me that I'd be speaking in the "black box." No, it's not what I thought. It was a very nice, small, and intimate auditorium, not much bigger than our St. Mark's Missionary Baptist Church.

In this setting, surrounded by the social issues of behavior challenges and self-indulgence, I would talk about my Delta porch people, their habits of unselfishness, and what those habits built and caused others to become.

The small auditorium was packed. It wasn't a mandatory parent assembly, but they came out in droves. They brought their children with them. I could tell it was going to be an exciting evening as I looked out on the sea of people who represented the world. It was truly an international evening. No matter where I stood, I was close to the people. My initial fears were soon put to rest as the audience grabbed each story as if it was their own. From the center of that small intimate auditorium, I told the stories of ordinary people who, because of their unselfish focus, became extraordinary leaders for me and for thousands of others who also were beneficiaries of their good acts.

They kept their eyes glued on me as I moved up and down the aisles, stopping and talking, asking questions and giving them a chance to respond. A few were so moved that they expressed their wish to have experienced the community I encountered. They wanted to know if their lives could be like that of my great-grandfather, who always shared his time with us. For me, though, the highlight was when a young boy defined his great moment of community as riding to the cheese markets on Saturday with his grandfather, just the two of them. We both had our "Poppa" stories. Love and unselfishness look and feel the same the world over. They were completely taken with Ma Ponk and her unfailing dedication. The evening was a success, and they were challenged to rethink their busy lives for the benefit of their children and the future that was unfolding before all of them. With the speech over, I had to get ready for the next day and the workshop where we were to dig deeper into the lives of the porch people.

I watched as my elders' front porches grew bigger and bigger and welcomed more and more people. Only God could have arranged such a gathering, and only He could have written and served up such a universal conversation. I gave Him my little bit and He did the rest.

Of all my trips, this one had bothered me. I thought our cultures to be too different for there to be a heartfelt connection. I was wrong. God knew His people. And I would witness even more the next day.

During the workshop the following day, we discussed all "Eight Habits of the Heart"—Nurturing Attitude, Responsibility, Dependability, Friendship, Brotherhood, High Expectations, Courage, and Hope, and personalized them as people I had known. I then gave out the first interactive assignment. I watched as several Chinese women searched the archives of their minds and several Catholic Sisters conversed and nodded in approval to each other as they talked among themselves about the concept of courage. I watched the Japanese attendees look deeply at their assignment sheets and at each other as they began the process of putting their thoughts on paper. From where I stood, I could see an Australian lady feverishly writing. She had immediately understood the assignment. A young man from New Zealand had not hesitated at all; he started his writing almost immediately as well. Apparently this assignment had resonated with him.

Finally, after I felt they had used all the time available, they were asked to share with all of us the look of courage and how it had been personalized in their lives. One by one, I listened as people of courage from around the world came to life through the memories of others. Their stories were all incredible and moving. Even though they were from around the world, they looked and felt like the people I experienced while growing up in Glen Allan. I was beginning to understand that unselfishness did indeed come from a deep well, one that was accessible all over the world.

God was validating for me that what I had given Him were testimonies of His presence that had been revealed in my life through the everyday actions of my porch people. And while here in Hong Kong with this international group of educators, many of whom were people of great faith, it was as if all our individual stories came from a common source.

However, I must tell you about a particular young man who personalized his vision of courage as I had done with my story. I'll never forget his story. "My Name Is Andrew" was the subject's headline. I was intrigued but unsure of where the courage would be in a headline that simply stated "My name is...." I asked the young man to stand and read aloud, and I am glad I did. It appears that a group of young New Zealand men, of which he was one, had spent their entire young lives together. They were fond of each other. However, among them was a rather small guy whom they simply called "Titch," which is a common nickname for small or tiny people never expected to get bigger. Without much thought, they all became comfortable calling their friend "Titch." As life goes, they all grew up and went away to college, and at some point during those years they decided to have a reunion. They wanted to see the old gang. They were all invited and all accepted. The reunion rolled around, and they were all together except for "Titch," who would be coming in on the train later that afternoon. So they all decided to go down to the train station to meet their buddy. When they saw him stepping from the train, they all very excitedly called out as they always had, "Titch, Titch, Titch," Without hesitation, for the very first time ever, he looked them in the eyes and very straightforwardly said, "My name isn't 'Titch'; it's Andrew."

In some real ways, many of us have faced similar situations where we have been defined by others. We have been called "Titch." "Titch," though, is not our name. Nor does it accurately describe who we are. We are the handiwork of God. And when we surrender to Him, He tells us who we are. And when He does, we marvel at how so little can mean so much.

I could personally identify with Andrew. I knew a whole race of people who could identify with "Andrew." While I was growing up in the South and certainly while my parents' generation was growing up, we all were subjected to mean-spirited names crafted by others and yelled out with venom. It took courage for "Andrew" to speak up in his situation, just as it did for all the people whose lives spoke up for me. Through their courageous living and abiding faith, I was able to tell the world that my name isn't "hey boy." I was shielded from so much. It must have been their "faith"; how else could they have loved so consistently?

My day ended, and we all hugged as if we were brothers and sisters. And in fact we were.

While they ate from my small meal, I also was able to eat from theirs. It had all been arranged. God allowed all of us to see and for many of us to experience what happens when ordinary people step up to do right things. My voice was becoming a catalyst for such conversations, and they were now taking place all over the world. My great-aunt wanted me to dig my way to China so that I would stay out of trouble, but God had plans for me to be in China to tell stories of those whose unselfish lives kept me from trouble.

From Sam, the young Chinese man who courageously drove us each day, to Mr. Chan and the hundreds of others I met, I can never forget being in a world I thought I'd never see. I was there simply because of His touch on my five loaves and two small fishes.

The cardboard box of short stories had now become four books, but I was still unable to see all that He would do. In God's plan, ordinary people are becoming international concepts. He's talking, and slowly I am beginning to listen.

Fragments From His Touch— Life Lessons to Pass Along

Never underestimate the weight of your words in the life of someone else. Remember, we are all the handiwork of God. And when we surrender our lives to Him, we see His creation from His perspective.

Chapter 13

GOD'S CHOSEN
PEOPLE IN MY STORY

Being in Hong Kong and being part of the conference on character was indeed extending the lessons of the Delta. I could no longer doubt that God was using their simple stories and my voice to accomplish a much bigger purpose. Only God could lay the groundwork for character education in the midst of racism and legal segregation. His touch made the difference, and because it did we have the account of the five loaves and the two fishes multiplied beyond the lunch packed for one.

Thousands of years later I was seeing the same thing. Because of one small book touched by God, timely concepts and international conversations were emerging, more books were pouring forth, and I was heading toward a destination determined by God—a destination that would eventually place me in the presence of His chosen people. Just as He knew China was in my future, God also knew that one day I would talk to Jews from Israel. He prepared me for that conversation when I was only ten years old with little or no knowledge of modern-day Israel. While going about my youthful routine in Glen Allan, God caused my heart to embrace an incident that would one day become an important story to the many Jewish people I would later meet. Yes, you are right. My very first book, *Once Upon a Time When We Were Colored*, and the book *Eight Habits of the Heart* caught the attention of a Jewish lady who at the time lived in Tulsa, Oklahoma. Sara became fascinated with the sense of community that I wrote and lectured about and invited me over the years to speak to the many Jewish groups who were official visitors to America and Tulsa.

Most of the times when I was invited to speak to the Jewish delegations, we always met at a home, the local library, or a designated public building. This time, however, was different. The meeting would not take place in a library or in the comfort of Sara's home, but in the local temple. I was honored that I was asked to address this group in the temple. I also was afraid. I had only been in the temple once, and it was to attend the funeral of one of Tulsa's well-known and respected business leaders so many years earlier. I remember being given the small skull cap and quietly walking in and sitting as close to the back as I could. I was in awe of this Jewish service because it was so different from the funerals remembered from my youth and from those held within the African-American community. After all those years, I was still in awe of the temple. And now I was being asked to join distinguished Jewish leaders as a speaker in the temple where I once quietly slipped in and sat close to the back. This time I would be seated up front and with me would be the family and friends from the Mississippi Delta, those ordinary people whose life stories had been touched by God. Now His chosen people would be fed from what He had touched.

The day that I was to speak, I made sure that I was on time and had with me all my lecture notes. And just as it was at the funeral many years earlier, a gentleman kindly fitted me with my skull cap, only this time I was unable to hide in the back. I was led to the front where I was seated. There, from my seat, I watched as our Jewish guests filed in. There were young men and young women. Even though their dress was no different than that of any other young people, I knew that they were from Israel, and that alone made the difference. Old men with white beards and distinguished frames walked to the front and faced me squarely. The women, dressed for travel, nodded and smiled. I was nervous. Some were speaking English with a distinct accent, while others were speaking Hebrew. I watched and listened, and the more I did, the more nervous I became. I was sitting up front and wearing a skull cap. I was not a rabbi. I looked at the people who were looking at me. I could only imagine their thoughts as I could see them whispering among themselves. I think I was the only non-Jewish person in the temple. Finally the time for the official program arrived. After the program was introduced, I sat quietly and listened as a distinguished Jewish lawyer spoke. Then it was my turn.

It seemed as if the temple became larger and the crowd even bigger. But I was prepared. My carefully prepared notes were with me. I listened as Sara introduced me. And when she beckoned for me, I stood. As I walked to the front, all my notes fell from my hands. I was truly nervous. Now I didn't know what to do. I quickly asked Sara and one other person to try and sort the papers and get me the section that contained my notes. They tried but were unable to help. I was lost, but God was not. As I was temporarily stunned, I quietly heard a small voice from deep within me saying, "Tell them the story."

I had no other choice but to take my audience to Glen Allan where God had already, some 35 years earlier, prepared my heart for this day.

While they looked at me, I listened to God. And from my small volume, I told them the story that introduced me to the heart of His people. Legal segregation was the law of the land and racial separation was almost always followed to the letter. The difference between the haves and the have-nots was obvious. Yet, this story of unselfishness took place at a time when it was much easier to maintain the status quo. God showed me a future in the home of a Southern Jewish lady that I would one day experience. When I started writing years ago, recalling the people who had positively impacted my life, Mrs. Freid was there among my porch people. This would be the story that I would tell in Temple Israel. As I talked, they all listened as the interior of the temple gave place to the heat and humidity of the Mississippi Delta.

Our guests had come from a war-torn land where kin were separated by wire fences and traditions. Death was commonplace, and the search for home was still a subject on the minds of many. They longed for community and relationships that were built on mutual respect. God had just the story for them. It was hard for me to imagine that an incident from Glen Allan, Mississippi, would one day ring out through a Jewish temple to God's chosen people.

"When I was a child, I knew very little about Judaism. The Star of David was quilts made by older 'colored' women who pieced them together from clothes no longer able to be worn. For me, the Judaism you embrace was a lady who lived out the love of God. We all knew her, but on this particular day I found myself outside my 'colored' neighborhood. I was uptown and close to the home of Mr. and Mrs. Freid, the owners of the local hardware store. I could see the pecan-covered yard from the road. I could see where I wanted to be, but we were separated by a wire fence and society. As a little kid, I stood on the outside and looked across to more than I had. I wanted in, but I knew I was in the wrong neighborhood. For me to be on her side of the fence would have helped an entire family. As was the custom in those days, children had to help earn money for the house, and picking pecans was one of the jobs we often had to do. I didn't mind it. I had done it all my life, but I had never picked pecans outside of the then 'colored' neighborhoods. From their windows, we could be seen looking and wishing, and it would have been easy for those on the inside to close their curtains to my needs and continue on with theirs. Fortunately for me and my cousin, tradition was interrupted, and before long we heard a voice of welcome that reached beyond the fence that separated our worlds.

"It was the voice of Mrs. Freid. From her window, she had seen us and with her heart she welcomed us in. She gave us, my cousin and me, permission to pick all the pecans we wanted. Her invitation rang clear, 'Boys, come on in.' She could have asked, 'What are you boys doing up here? Aren't you out of your neighborhood? Now y'all go on back home.' Instead, she beckoned for us to come in. She was moved with compassion, not guided by tradition.

Without hesitation, we jumped the side fence and before long we were picking as many pecans as we wanted. While we were picking pecans, our efforts were soon interrupted by the strong smells of food making its way into the pecan orchard. And the stronger the smell, the closer we moved to the house. We must have been a sight to see because, before long, Miss Hester, the cook, was calling us in for lunch. The call that brought us to the orchard was not expected. And now this call to eat in the house and not be given a sandwich from the back door was made into the story that I am now telling.

"We were being invited into a white home. Something lived in that house that even allowed the hired help to be generous in invitation and voice. Miss Hester, sticking her head out of the back kitchen door, laughed as she called us in. We knew the custom, and we were prepared to go through the back door. That would have been the custom, but that day, many traditions were being broken and community was being built. Before we had a chance to contemplate our response, Mrs. Freid was at the side door, not the back door, but the side door, waiting to show us in. It was as if it was only yesterday. I can still see her with her crinkly hair pulled tightly back, wearing a gray sweater, a flowered print dress, with her comfortable shoes, and her arms folded, welcoming us into her home and through her husband's study where we no doubt tracked mud on her hardwood floor, but it didn't seem to matter. She wasn't given to much conversation, but the warmth of the welcome was genuine. Even as a little boy, I knew that it was all right to be in her home. We were ushered onto tall bar stools, the first I had seen, and plates of food were placed in front of us. This is where I was first introduced to matzo ball soup. It looked strange to me, and the taste did not alter my opinion. The matzo ball soup I didn't take to, but the kosher salami sandwich still tastes good when eaten with a thick slice of homemade angel food cake and washed down with a cold glass of sweet milk. Sitting at her kitchen counter and treated as any young child should be treated will always be remembered. Her courageous unselfishness stood out when racism and bigotry defined our worlds. Mrs. Freid's kindness was the Judaism I first encountered."

In this story of the two women, I was allowed to see how traditional position and place of separation and power could be overcome by courageous friendship—a friendship that changed both women as they carved out a world among themselves behind their curtains, a place where the kitchen table became both their temples of friendship. As I think about the actions of the heart of these two ladies in their highly segregated world, I remember how they nodded to each other and made sure that we felt no ill will for being there. I was a beneficiary of the largess of their hearts, and after I finished eating I went home with plenty of fresh pecans and a story that God would later use to talk to His people.

That day in Temple Israel, the silence was spiritual. No sounds other than my voice could be heard as their eyes fastened on me and their ears tuned in to the unique sounds from the Mississippi Delta. In this simple story told in their temple, they remembered the strength of their faith and recalled the generosity of their God. I was not a rabbi, but a message had been delivered from the side door of a Jewish home many years ago. When Sara came to the podium to thank me, she asked the delegation's leader for his response. He was seated on the front row, stately and looking as I would think Moses may have looked. He stood and with tears and a choked voice simply said, "How can I talk with my heart so full?" The day I shared this story in the Jewish temple—Temple Israel—will always be remembered. I left the temple that day no longer intimidated but filled with the knowledge that I felt the presence of Jehovah God in Temple Israel.

I don't know if the story had great meaning when it actually happened. I know I took the pecans home and that I left Mrs. Freid's kitchen with a full stomach of kosher food. However, when the story was called for by God, it became more than a simple memory of a young boy who grew up in Mississippi. It became a parable for a nation looking for peace and a place to call home.

The Jewish delegation returned to Israel, but others would come. They too would hear the same story, and it would be as if it had never been told before. It was as fresh for the new ears as the dew that descends from the mountains. However, the response of the Magen David Adom delegation further validated the power of God to make much out of little and to continue feeding from the same stock.

These Jewish men and women and several very young volunteering adults had come to America as part of an exchange studying the role of the Red Cross in various domestic incidences of violence. Again, it was Sara who asked me to speak. I was honored to do so. Though I can't pronounce their names, I felt as if they were right out of the Old Testament; names like Gilad, Yossi, Siglit, Menachem, Ammon, and Aviva.

They understood how I felt at being invited into Mrs. Freid's house. For many of them, they or members of their immediate family had at one time stood on the outside of Israel and looked in. My story of feeling isolated from plenty was not unusual to them. However, because they were volunteer firemen who volunteered across ethnic lines, I also felt the need to take them further into the "colored" neighborhood with the story of a fire that almost destroyed all our homes had not the "whites" and "coloreds" put aside their biases, fears, and mistrust of each other and worked together.

Both my head and heart were full as I thought about the day when the story was reality. I could hardly wait to take them to the place where I had seen unselfish actions being lived out across social and racial lines. I can still hear the screaming as the word spread that Miss Shugg Payne's house was on fire. Our small town had no fire truck. We only had each other and an old water pump that was located in the yard of the white family who lived across the road from the burning house.

Everybody who lived down by the "colored" school had to work together to put it out, both blacks and whites. I was small, but I remember my great-aunt out front leading the way and calling for others to come along. Though I was too young to be of much help, I was right there running as fast as I could across the "colored" school yard with my great-aunt, watching the crowds gather and the human line form. The flames were leaping into the air and billows of black smoke could be seen everywhere. I watched as both races formed a human water line, sweating and working together. I remembered how my great-aunt shoved me into the line even though I was little. My hands did touch the buckets as they passed by me. For a few moments race did not matter; we all were doing what was right for one another.

The quietness in the room sounded like peace. They knew of such moments. They had seen Jews and Muslims working together, just as I had witnessed both races from my community becoming brothers and sisters during the crisis, but afterwards returning to their separate worlds where fear and mistrust again became the order of the day.

Another parable from Glen Allan for God's people had just been shared. How much could come from such a small place? It was just a fire near the "colored" school, but I was there. I observed the courage and the hope that only we can provide each other. It was so long ago it should have been forgotten, but it was called up late one night when my fear of war and death hung over my head. God called for this story, and I wrote it, not knowing that one day it would be a parable of peace and community for His people.

After I finished, no one wanted to talk. Finally, Gilgad, one of their spokespersons, came up front where I was standing and thanked me on behalf of the group for telling the story of courage, hope, and unselfishness during a very difficult time. Gilgad and I just looked at each other, then politely shook hands, but that was not enough. When you share hearts, more is required. Tears began to fall and became like rain running down our cheeks, salty and wet, becoming one stream. We then tightly embraced and held on to each other as we said nothing but understood deeply what had taken place. We acknowledged our common heritage. We all were children of God.

I know now that my life is being directed by God in a way I never imagined. Yet, even with this knowledge, I am not at ease with the assignment. Still, I continue, and so does God.

Fragments From His Touch— Life Lessons to Pass Along

Two parables were shared with the people of God. Both were from the Mississippi Delta, a long ways from Israel, but close to the heart of God. From those simple parables, God again showed His people the possibilities of brotherhood. I was there and watched the courage, the hope, and the brotherhood we can provide to each other. Both parables happened long ago, but they were not forgotten. Our lives, lived out and passed along, continue to be parables for others.

Chapter 14

FRAGMENTS FEEDING THE NEXT GENERATION

Even though by now I have four books to my credit, my first book, the one that grew out of hundreds of rejected short stories, continues to amaze me. Without question that little book has God's touch on every page, and He continues to feed from the lessons therein. God's continued feeding gives overwhelming support to the fragments gathered by His disciples. This time, though, the fragments are not in 12 baskets, but in thousands of literature textbooks for young middle school students throughout America. Yes, you are reading correctly; my little late-night writings caught the eyes of a major textbook publisher who then excerpted a chapter from my book, *Once Upon a Time When We Were Colored,* for inclusion in the McDougal Littrel Literature for middle schools. Now children throughout America have the opportunity to taste from the lunch of simple stories that has become an international conversation on building community.

Today God continues His hand in our lives as He expects us to continue to be the hands and hearts in the lives of children who cross our paths. Without being valued as a child by the adults who crossed my path, I would not have these stories to share nor have any fragments for future generations. This is the beauty of God. He does show up, even in the Mississippi Delta, and when He finds willing hearts, His touch still takes our little and makes much.

I had no idea that my elders would still be talking to young people around the world. I had no idea that the book that held their lives would one day rise to a position of prominence in the literary world and be excerpted in middle school literature books throughout America—and in many cases become required reading for social studies and as a first-person companion to American history. Well, it did, and because of that, young minds throughout this country have been exposed to the undeniable role of unselfishness that is just as needed today as it was when I was growing up.

Needless to say, I was delighted to learn of the excerpt, but it was not until I received a large shoebox filled with letters from middle school students from a school in Utah that I truly realized just how much God had done. The day I got that large shoebox, I realized that hearts were being changed and that my stories were part of the process.

The students at first had only one story from the book, just the fragments, but from that taste they embarked upon a bigger journey that would take them deep inside a community where unselfishness flourished and that refused to allow racism and bigotry to define how they lived within their homes and how they took care of their children. They could see the impact of my elders upon my life, but they also became challenged to think of their roles during their generation to build a better society. They were reading, but the heart of God was talking, just as He had talked at Glen Mary's Plantation...reminding me of the possibilities of how pleasant it is when brethren dwell together in unity.

The shoebox that introduced me to those who were feasting from the fragments of God's touch arrived several years ago, but the incident is still fresh in my mind and will no doubt remain so. On this particular day I went to the mailbox as usual but noticed that the metal mailbox door was wide open. I was about to get upset at the postal person. Then I thought that maybe my mailbox was full of mail. The problem was not much mail, but a large shoebox mashed down, badly bruised, and addressed to me. After tugging to get it out, I shook it, tossed it in the air, and reread the label to make sure it bore my name. It did, and it was correctly spelled. The box was held together by duct tape, which gave cause for suspicion. I didn't know anyone in Utah, but my name was boldly on the label. Who could be sending me something from Utah? I couldn't wait to get inside and show this mutilated box to my wife.

"Barbara, you will not believe this," I yelled as I entered the house. "We got a shoebox of something." "Be careful," she called back. "You can never tell what people will do these days. Take it in the kitchen!" I laughed. For Barbara, the mysterious box momentarily brought "shades of terrorism," but I'm not really well enough known for her to worry. Nevertheless, I went straight to the kitchen as I was told and dropped the mystery box on the self-serve island. But before I could say anything more, I heard Barbara coming down the hall. She was curious too, and I guessed we were going to open the box together.

After shaking it one more time, I got a pair of scissors and cut the twine and duct tape that held the box together. Ripping into the box, I was amazed to find this large stack of handwritten letters. Upon close examination and with a nicely written letter from the teacher, I learned that the box of letters were from eighth-grade students in West Jordan, Utah. I'll never understand how they got so many letters into that one small box. After looking at each letter individually and admiring the accompanying pictures the students had drawn, I read the nicely written letter from the teacher explaining the wonderful story behind this box of letters.

Anni Bjerke, a young teacher who had crossed my path in Tulsa many years before when we were members of the same church, now taught middle school in this small Utah community. To help her students reflect on "Black Life: Past and Present," she had introduced her class to the excerpt and the book, *Once Upon a Time When We Were Colored*. After having read the book and viewed the movie, Anni's students were given an additional opportunity to write me and ask me questions about the world I called home.

God cared about the next generations, the ones that followed my own. I could see that as I read the letters from each student. They were thoughtful and insightful and many of them expressed changed per-

spectives after having spent time in the lives of the people I knew and loved. They felt the sting of racism leaping from the pages and from the screen, and in their letters their young hearts promised to live their lives differently. I trust that they will; their generation and this century will need hearts and minds willing to live by God's best desires for all of us.

For many of these young people, to study my life and those of the porch people was equal to taking a foreign history course. It wasn't foreign, though; it was their story too. As Americans, we were so close but yet so very far away. God allowed me to write these stories in a way that narrowed the distance between our separate lives. Now I look back and understand that God was planning this book all along, providing me the love and care and a front porch from where I would see and feel unselfishness and faithfulness in spite of the reality of racism and discrimination. God allowed me to write what was lasting: His presence in our lives.

I could tell from their letters that in reading the book and watching the movie, they had run into the sting of racism. But as God would have me only tell it, they also saw how, through the help of others, the poison was taken out of the sting. In a very subtle way, they were being shown what could be expected of them. I could tell they identified with me, the young boy, and my hurt became their hurt and my joy became their joy as well.

These young people and their letters, as it turned out, were very insightful, honest, and even funny as they found themselves in my great-grandfather's car, at church, or having a great Southern meal.

These are conversations from their letters. (For the sake of these children's privacy, I am not including their names.)

One of the letter writers who had watched the movie and read the book recognized the difficulty in growing up and working for people who had no respect for your skills and life. Not only did she focus on this, but she also said, "If I were there when they treated you like that, I would have tried to stop it." Even today, we still need people like this young lady who can see wrong and act to end it. A boy drew a picture of the "w" and the "c" in a scene from the movie where Poppa Joe, my great-grandfather, was teaching me the difference between "white" and "colored." His letter was very straightforward, sharing what he had learned about racism and how he admired me—which of course meant that he also admired the strength of the people whose lives were shaping my very own.

Another young correspondent drew a wonderful picture of me on a train leaving home. Yet, she wanted to know how was I able to keep such a positive attitude and not hate many of my white neighbors. She asked if, as an adult, I have white friends. "Love your neighbor as yourself" hasn't changed; as a Christian I am expected to embrace this commandment. And I do. Would I have been able to do so had I not been surrounded by those whose faith shaped their attitudes? Today I can say that my circle of friends has expanded and continues to do so as people of all races cross my path. While reading this student's well-written letter and looking at the beautiful picture of a train moving into a world where the sun is shining and all the trees are green, I wanted her to know that I learned not to hate because God had already shown the adults around me the tragedy of such feelings, and they had passed His teachings on to me.

When I read the letter from another young man, I both laughed and cried. He wanted to know if our homes were cold in the winter. These kinds of thoughts cross your mind when you realize that you are connected to the person in the picture and want for that person what you want for yourself. He knew his life and wondered if my life had afforded me a good bed. Seeds of unselfishness were being planted in his young heart, and hopefully he'll grow up and continue along this path. That's what this boy wanted for me, and I trust that his heart will retain such sensitivity for as long as he shall live, so that others may see this good act lived out in him.

Another student drew a picture that just captured Poppa and me. Her view of Poppa's car was a bit futuristic, but she captured his love and care and my feeling of comfort. Just as it was important for me to run into love and care in the midst of legal segregation, so it was also important for these young people to see the impact of goodness and perhaps be challenged to be the "good" themselves as we all should and as my porch people so graciously did. Her letter reminded me that strength and love can live in the same body, an observation that must not be lost on this generation.

Nearly every letter I read from these bright Utah students seemed to question the lack of anger. One girl said, "If they [the whites] did that to me, I'd really be mad." I don't know how she did it, but Ma Ponk took the sting out of the bite because she had allowed God, early on, to mold and shape her attitude. She was neither asleep nor unmindful of the ill treatments suffered; she just chose to live her life in not seeking revenge. I learned from her that vengeance does belong to God. God showed her His way, and like I said, she passed it on. Somehow, as people, we can do that for each other. However, when I read the letter from another young girl, I realized that generations of Americans were growing up with little or no knowledge of the burdens that slavery and legal segregation placed upon our lives. "What was it like to live like you did?" She wanted an interior view of our world, and I was able to provide it for her in the book that came to me at night while in the military.

Another eighth grader, though only 14 at the time he wrote, offered some mature observations that I hope will always be part of who he is. "I feel bad that people were that close-minded that they couldn't see past skin color to the person underneath." I feel bad too, but I still have hope. We must believe in tomorrow, going beyond what we see because of the deeper insights of our hearts, and I want him to know that his dream must be for the world. From Israel to the Congo, from L.A. to Harlem, from Appalachia to our Mississippi Delta, we must find ways to embrace what is common and universal among all of us because it is good when brethren dwell together in unity.

When I read this student's letter, it was clear that she recognized how people were able to share their lives, protect their families, and provide vision for the future. She simply said, "I learned that money isn't everything." I'm so glad she recognizes that a dollar strategically placed is no substitute for caring. She saw and felt the impact of the community who shared their lives with me. I needed them to stop and invest in my life, and we need to do the same in the lives of children all over the world. How do we know where the next transforming book is being shaped? We don't, but we can plan to be available and ready.

This next student writer was not one to mince words. "I learned that racism stinks." Another young man also recognized this and told me so in his letter. As he read the book and watched the movie, he became "me" for a moment in time and felt the sting of the insults. He wanted to fight back and questioned my inner feelings. I would tell him what I tell you: Vengeance does not belong to me; nor do I have the strength to bear its weight. One student suggested that we reverse history so that whites will know the sting of racism. We know we can't, and I would choose not to do that. However, in her eighth-grade mind, she no doubt feels that if we walk a mile in another's shoes, we'll get the picture of what is required to bolster and appreciate our shared humanity.

One young man was only 12 when he wrote me. Though he now lives in Utah, he's from Ecuador, in South America, a long, long way from the Mississippi Delta. I wish that many adults could view the world from his young perspective: "I learned that you need to have respect for everyone, and not judge someone for his or her skin color. I learned that being poor isn't the end of your life." And it certainly isn't, when the richness of our faith-relationships continues to change circumstances and provide hope and vision.

An Asian boy reminded me of the universality of our daily living. He asked the type of questions we ask when we have accepted the fact of our kinship. Growing up, though, I never thought my life would be interesting to others like these inquisitive eighth graders. Yet, 40 years later, my small world has indeed expanded to the generation of young people who will one day lead us. Hopefully their leading will be reflective of unselfishness and caring and they'll have a better understanding of what is expected of them as a result of their historic journey into the pages of a small book.

Maybe this is why Jesus asked us to make way for the children to know Him. Don't stand in their way. Their tender hearts must always be fed with what He has touched. Through them, this creation continues to have opportunities to live out God's dream for us.

I can only stand and stagger at all that God has done. From a series of short stories, He has opened up a dialogue with the world. I am humbled to be on this journey with Him, but I still find reason to question it all.

Fragments From His Touch— Life Lessons to Pass Along

Our children must see our right acts if they are to know what is expected of them. We are our brother's keeper, and there is great joy in fulfilling that role. Our God knows the joy of community, and throughout His Word we are challenged to dwell together in unity and experience the joy of being a precious ointment.

Chapter 15

DISCOVERING MY PLACE...A CONTINUOUS JOURNEY

After seeing images of my picture books for children being read by American servicemen to young children in the marketplaces of Iraq, I knew that God had indeed touched my words for such a time as this. The accolades for my literary journey are numerous, and I have embraced them all. What started out as stories in the night are now recognized as timeless and universal principles to build and for some to re-build community. This conversation resonated with audiences around the world, but it also brought me back to the heart of the Delta as concerned citizens within the academic world sought ways to lift the eyesight of those less fortunate and to revitalize the Delta I once called home.

These lessons of community had always been present in the Delta. I saw them throughout the small "colored" communities when I was growing up. The broader community overlooked them as non-essential to their way of life. And unfortunately, many of us set them aside as integration and the challenges and opportunities of the 1960's came into our lives. God, however, did not forget them. Those good acts were His doings. I had seen them and remembered them. He asked for them, and now after years of travel and recognition around the world, the lessons from the front porches of our lives are being welcomed home.

So great were the concerns for the economy and for ways to better the lives of the citizens that I along with others were called to come home to Delta State University to attend a symposium where the future of the Delta would be explored through literature and conversation. Had I not written, I would not have been part of this call. Because God allowed me to write a book laced with hope and promise, I was called to help rekindle minds and hearts of all the citizens to look beyond their historical past of separatism to build a new and inclusive future.

God brought me back to where I had started not only to show me the truth of His presence in my life, but also to speak hope to others whose lives were not too different than the one I knew so well. I would tell them that I knew a community of people who left for all of us a legacy of survival and hope that lived beyond what was actually seen.

I arrived in Cleveland, Mississippi, in the pouring rain and could hardly wait for the next morning when I would speak to this gathering of Southerners who had come home to address both our social and economic needs. The next morning was abuzz with activity as the auditorium filled up. It was indeed a wonderful sight. I was seated on stage, and after the introductory remarks were made I was introduced by Pamela Moore of Oxfam America. Reverend Moore is an incredible lady and as a Methodist preacher had served as an itinerant minister at the Allan Chapel AME Church in my hometown of Glen Allan. While serving in Glen Allan, she ran into remnants of that indomitable spirit of survival still lingering amidst the aged, the wearied, and the worn. She completed her talk and welcomed me home and to the podium.

I would give them the truth of what I had witnessed: simple lives with powerful messages. The lives of the poor people who had been overlooked and undervalued had now become parables for the very people who had passed them by. Had not God called their lives to my attention, I too may have looked over them and discounted all that they had done for my generation and beyond.

I knew that this would be a time to talk to the audience as one people. It was not a time to use my voice to verbally right a wrong but to listen closely to God and His heart for all those assembled. God had been an integral part of my life on the Delta and was without question responsible for whatever upward mobility that had come my way. These listeners were looking for answers. They wanted to know if survival could happen again. As I talked, I felt as if I was small once again, experiencing God's love that showed up

163

in the people who chose to stop and live beyond their personal agendas. The word pictures took them into the same front rooms that thousands had visited in the book. As I talked, I could see their faces and could see them slowly coming home with me. It was if the stories I told were now becoming a healing place for others.

Surrounded by representatives from the Jewish, Chinese, black, white, and Italian communities, a Southern gathering that I had not witnessed in my lifetime, I humbly and carefully took them along the road where I could have been left alone and into the lives of the people who were determined not to leave me where they found me. I talked with them about the maids, the field hands, the tractor drivers, the preachers, and the few teachers whose daily unselfishness became the story that they, along with others, had come to embrace and the dynamics that emerged from what seems simple...the timeless power of building relationships between people. As I took them from home to church and back to home again, it seemed as if I could hear the voices from back home, "Tell them to focus on the people." I knew this to be the right thing to do and the right thing for me to say; after all, for me it was their generation, many of whom I never encountered, who fashioned emotional change and transformation for me by building a caring community—right in the midst of their personal disenfranchisement, not unlike the hard times these listeners now faced in the Delta. The audience heard my words, but I also felt as if all my elders had gathered there with me to cheer me on. God knew their lives would be lessons of value, and once again others were experiencing what God always knew.

*People were now saying that I was "called" to do what I had been doing for nearly ten years—not just people with a religious inclination, but others as well. In my lecture sessions, people are moved, sometimes to tears, but always to great appreciation for the stories that challenged their behavior. It was as if my life had moved beyond being a professional lecturer. I had never forgotten what had happened in Las Vegas. I just kept it to myself. Was I "called" to do this? I wasn't sure. The word **called** scared me, and I was unsure of my ability to live up to the expectations associated with such a powerful word.*

The light we bring to the darkness often comes in the form of stories individually experienced to be collectively shared. The Delta has fallen on hard times, but I think, like my life and that of countless others who lived through and beyond legal segregation, it can come back. The soil of our daily living is still rich. It has always been the crops we planted that defined our harvest.

God gave the porch people a message. I wrote their story. I became their voice. I left Cleveland, Mississippi, and returned to Tulsa where my schedule kept me traveling. Fortune 500 companies had embraced my teachings on "leadership," which also had emerged from the same stories I had first written some 34 years earlier. I was being introduced as a "thought-leader" on the issues of community. CNN had featured me on their Millennium Minute Series as a representative of community. Little had become much. And I was on my way to further establishing my roots in corporate America and around the world.

While on my way to corporate success, I suffered a heart attack in the Tulsa International Airport. Once more it seemed as if all that I had come to love was gone. I couldn't understand why this had happened to me. What would my clients do? What if I died? During this time in my life I faced a personal fear that no one could share. I had to bear this burden all alone. Or at least I thought I did. While in this state of distress and fear, the God I knew from Glen Allan showed up.

A young preacher and a graduate of Oral Roberts University, Jerome Steele, came to pray with me. As he prayed, I began to sob heavy wet tears that clung to my face. However, as each tear fell from my eyes, I also felt the fear go away. By the time the prayer and conversation were over, so was the fear that had gripped my heart. I was able to move beyond the fear that had gripped me. Light had entered my spirit, and I felt as if He was in the hospital room with me. As I lay there listening to the prognosis and being told by my nurse that even my exploratory test could end in death, I was at the same time being cradled by God. I heard the nurse, but I was seeing God. I don't recall any dramatic conversation or dancing lights or voices that boomed from the ceiling, but in my spirit, somewhere deep within me, I was feeling as if God had my full attention.

The required test validated that I had indeed suffered a heart attack, but the cardiologists were somewhat baffled when they looked inside of me and found only a very small artery at the back of my heart to have been damaged. According to them, my heart was strong and no deposits were seen in my arteries. I was slowed down. I had to listen. God had called me, and I now knew that I could no longer put Him off. I had to accept that my life had purpose within His plan. My becoming an author was no literary accident. It was part of God's plan, the part that I had enjoyed and embraced, but I was now beginning to see that writing and lecturing to professionals around the world was only part of the journey. His full plan would include more.

*Weeks and months passed, and I found myself gaining strength. While in the hospital and then recovering at home, I was surrounded by prayer. I was going to live and not die. It would seem that my first order of business would have been making sure that I was at the center of God's will for my life; instead, I was headed back to being the voice of community. Surely this would please God. Just talking about community and such good topics should have been all He required of me. I would later learn that God was requiring **all** of me and that His definition of availability and being ready were far different than my own. I started reading the Bible every day. This had not been a practice of mine. I was still afraid and wanted to make sure that God had my back. I was reading out of fear, not out of my great love, but I was in the Word.*

My first speech after the heart attack was in Moorehead, Minnesota. Going back to the airport for the first time since the heart attack was a bit unnerving, but I made it through security and on to my destination. It was freezing cold, colder than I had ever experienced. On the morning of my speech, ice and snow were everywhere. I was scheduled to speak in the college gym, and the entire Moorehead community, which is predominately white, had been invited to hear this African-American speak. I didn't think anyone would show up, but that morning before I left for the engagement, I spent hours reading the Word and was almost late for my ride due to reading the Bible. Now this was a first for me.

When I got to my destination, the place was packed. I was overwhelmed. They had come to feast from this small Southern lunch. What was I really going to say? I was ushered off to a side room where I had some quiet time, and it was during this time that I felt I was to write three words on a sheet of paper: "Imagine the Possibilities." I had never used those words before to start a speech. When I walked out, the place had no seats left. As I was being introduced, I felt with certainty that God was present. I listened as He used my voice to stretch their thinking about building community and the role of unselfishness. The place was so quiet it was as if the presence of angels were there. My mind had never been so clear, and it was as if I had never had the heart attack incident. The audience stood and cheered as I finished, and their handshakes were strong and warm.

*This was not the first time that I had experienced God's presence in one of my lectures, but this was the first time that I actually felt that maybe I **was** "called" to this job. Their response was beyond expectations, as were the write-ups in the paper the next day and the letters to the local editor that followed. For months afterwards, I'd look back on this event and think about the scripture reading the morning of the speech. Maybe I did have two jobs in one.*

From Minnesota to the U.S. Department of Justice, to the Island of Bermuda to the United States Air Force Academy, the "leadership" conversation was still in demand and I was trying my best to fulfill each call. I was still recovering but finding levels of weakness in my body that could not be explained. I had to stay in the presence of God. I was being forced to read the Word and pray, and in so doing my life was changing. My life had been altered on more than one level. Through all this change and clear understanding that God was in the mix of my life, I had refused to speak in churches. I would do everything I could to say no. I loved God, but I was still dealing with the issue of being "called." Also, unlike Daniel, I was afraid and embarrassed for my friends in "high places" to see me publicly honoring my God. I had made incredible and important friends around the world. I can actually pick up the phone and call Hollywood producers. I know the CEOs of Fortune 500 companies. Many of these people I now consider personal friends. I didn't want to lose them. What will they think of me? I wanted God to be happy with my private devotions and my public professionalism, separate but equal.

My speaking around the country continued, but my not speaking in churches would soon change. God used Pastor Billy Joe Daugherty of Tulsa, Oklahoma, to facilitate my change of heart. While at a civic event, Pastor Billy Joe invited me to speak at his church. At first I said no. But he convinced me that the conversation on community was just as viable for the church as it was for those in business. I could feel God breathing down my neck as well, so I said yes. The Sunday I spoke for Pastor Billy Joe, I understood through their ministry to me that my life would no longer only be on the side of business and commerce, but that the stories from my life were touched by God to feed all His people. I realized that I would stand in both arenas as Daniel had done.

I heard Pastors Billy Joe and his wife Sharon, but one day when I was home from travel and on the treadmill, I personally heard from God. I will not forget that day. I was sweaty and focused on finishing, when seemingly out of nowhere I heard these words: "I have built your résumé for My glory." I burst into tears and ran faster and faster. God had gotten my attention. I could no longer dictate how I would serve Him. He had been making plans for me since the day I was born. He had salvaged my life. And in that short period of time while on the treadmill in tears, He took me back to Dow Air Force Base at the time when most of my friends from my barracks were being shipped off to Viet Nam. I had so much to be thankful for, but over the course of time I had overlooked some of what God had done. He, though, had not forgotten. As He talked to my spirit, I remembered all. I knew the exact day when I was walking from my job and stopped by the barrack's bulletin board. I never stopped to read the bulletins because they usually came from administration, where I worked. That day I did. I didn't know why at the time, but now I do.

That day I focused on a small newspaper clipping. He reminded me of how I looked at the notice requesting applications for a job in a top-secret position in Washington, D.C. and said under my breath that I would never be considered for such an assignment. I actually applied with full knowledge that I'd never be chosen. Thousands applied for that same position. God chose me. Instead of being shipped off to Viet Nam, I went to Washington to the 89th Presidential Wing. I belonged to Him, and I knew that day while on the treadmill that He was calling in His chips.

My work, lectures, and workshops on leadership and building community continue, and so do my prayer and reading of the Word. I am still scared and not sure of where it's all leading to, but I do know for sure that God is leading. My humanity faces me each day. I am still trying not to relive Peter's big denial scene.

Privately, I have said yes. I thought I really meant it at the time. God tested my yes. I was at a holiday book signing in December of 2004 at one of the national bookstores. Everything was going well. I was happy. My wife was with me. People were buying books, and I was just signing away when a very well-dressed and important lady came up and asked about my next speaking gig. I thought for a moment. **I'll be speaking in Louisville, Kentucky, at a church.** *I didn't want to say that. I was embarrassed. So I just said that I'd be in Louisville, Kentucky. She was not satisfied. This lady was born in Louisville and wanted to know exactly where I'd be speaking. God put me on the spot.*

I finally eased out the name of the church, World Prayer Center, and the location. As she walked away, God talked. I almost denied Him. I understood that part of His requirements would be my great joy in serving Him and honoring Him no matter where I was or who I was facing. I asked for forgiveness and promised to be quick and forthright going forward. Please pray that I keep my promise. I now understand Peter. It's really easy sometimes to say, "I am not with Him."

I remind myself daily that all this is God's doing, not my own. I laugh with my friends as I tell them the difficulty I face as I walk into His plan that is continuously being revealed and requiring all of me.

As I close out the last chapter of this book, which is growing out of the same stories that God asked me to give Him in 1965, I take notice that I stopped in the middle of my writing this morning to hold a long-distance international conversation with a businessman in Germany. We talked about the community I encountered on the Mississippi Delta and the principles for sound business that emerged from that humble world. When we finished our conversation, I laughed to myself as I thought of what I had given God and what He in turn had allowed me to enjoy. I gave God all that I had, as small as it was and as overlooked as it had been, and yet with His touch little became much—12 baskets of leftovers and more—now feeding more than I imagined but also helping me to understand my place in all of this. My place, it seems, is simply to be available to God—putting His plan first, and as best I can living my life so that my availability also means that when called to action on His behalf, I am ready, prepared, and willing.

Thank you for making this journey with me. Obviously if you have read this book, you too are part of His plan for my life.

Fragments From His Touch—
Life Lessons to Pass Along

When we give ourselves to God, we also must be prepared for what His touch will do in our lives. I gave Him a few stories, and He wrote books and provided me a conversation that resonates around the world. Now I am challenged to give Him my commitment to His service. This will require prayer and reading the Word, both of which I was rather inconsistent doing. But both will transform our character, and that is essential if we are to be available, ready, and willing for His long-range plans for our lives. Our God is still asking us to bring our five loaves and our two fishes and to join Him in feeding those who hunger and thirst after righteousness.

ABOUT THE AUTHOR

Clifton LeMoure Taulbert, Pulitzer-nominated author and international lecturer, was born in the Mississippi Delta at the end of World War II in the home of his great-grandparents, Reverend Joe and Pearl Young. Later he went to live with his great-aunt Elna, and it was from her small front room window that he saw the world and within her small bedroom that he experienced her faith.

Clifton entered the military in 1964, eventually serving in the 89th Presidential Wing. He started his writing career while in the military during the Viet Nam war. His first book was published in 1989. *Once Upon a Time When We Were Colored* became an international success and was made into a motion picture that won the 1996 NAACP Image Award. His second book, *The Last Train North*, was nominated for the Pulitzer Prize and was one of Doubleday's Discovery Book of the Year. It also was the first book by an African-American to win the Mississippi Institute of Arts and Letters Award for Non-Fiction. Clifton's third book, *Watching Our Crops Come In*, was hailed by *The L.A.*

Times as required reading for all Americans. *Eight Habits of the Heart* was named by *USA TODAY* as their year-end choice of books to enrich our minds and lives.

Clifton Taulbert has lectured and held workshops on leadership, community, and character development all over the globe in the education, business, and church sectors. He also founded the Building Community Institute to extend the reach of the timeless and universal values encountered during his youth and that permeate his stories.

He won the Richard Wright Literary Award of Excellence and produced three picture books for children called *The Little Cliff Series—A Focus on Family & Extended Relationships*, which news broadcasts showed American soldiers reading to Iraqi children.